MW00849727

ADDICTION CONNECTION DISL

The Title and Story of this book is NOT intended to imply that there is a correlation between Tattoos and Substance Abuse Addiction or Addiction of Any Kind. It is the telling of my personal story, of the recognition of my addictive tenancies. When seen by me in hindsight, they began when I first ventured into some addictive behavior while chasing my very first tattoo. I reveal where I was physically, relationally, emotionally, and spiritually throughout the journey of my Tattoos. I tell my story with the hope of helping others, quite possibly yourself or a loved one, find not only the beginning, but the middle, and most importantly, the end to the most personal debilitating addictions. With the hope and belief that one day soon you will hear from your own lips or from those of a loved one, the same truth that came from mine, "I Survived The Perfect Storm Of Addiction."

Cody Lanus 2021

ADDICTION RECOVERY DISCLAIMER:

The publishing of Cody's Journey is NOT intended to be a stand in for, or a replacement of the Addiction Recovery Programs and Services offered by professionals in that field. Our hope is that it will serve, where 'Called', as a Powerful Prerequisite for and/or Addition to those very programs. We will Trust God to Guide you in your direction.

PriscillAquila Press 2021

TATTOOS

MY GATEWAY DRUG

SURVIVING THE
PERFECT STORM
OF ADDICTION

CODY LANUS
WITH GARY MARTEL

Tattoos, My Gateway Drug
Surviving The Perfect Storm Of Addiction
Copyright @2021 by Cody Lanus with Gary Martel

Published by:
PriscillAquila Press
213 Churment Court
Durham NC 27703
www.PriscillAquila.com

PriscillAquila
Press

Print ISBN: 978-1-7370033-1-1
eBook ISBN: 978-1-7370033-2-8
Library of Congress Control Number: 2021939203

Editor: GJ Martel / ES Parker
Cover & Interior Design: Fusion Creative Works, fusioncw.com

Printed in the United States of America
First Edition

For my Grandparents
Bob and Donna

I lost sight of the recipe you showed me,
and then I found it once again:

simple, kind, and faithful.

This book is for you.

CONTENTS

ACKNOWLEDGEMENTS

First and foremost I would like to say, "Without God's guidance, this book would have simply remained an idea." You will soon discover why.

This book is unique. Not only was it written in prison, but it was also done so without the luxuries of modern assistance like Office Word. That created many challenges on my end. Every page was handwritten, self-edited, re-written, typed via prison email system, sent, and edited by Gary, then edited by Ellen, emailed back to me, printed in the prison library, re-read, and repeating that cycle many times all over again. Furthermore, to get the full manuscript back to me to proofread in its totality, was a challenge itself. The prison only allows 5 single-sided pieces of paper per envelope. To say there were a handful of hurdles would be a massive understatement.

Secondly, I would like to personally thank those mentioned above. Gary Martel wore many hats during the process of this project: co-author, editor, mentor, therapist, chaplain, drug-counselor, and friend. It was a vision he had, that brought this book to life and his diligence, that saw it through. He turned raw emotion into structure, for which the foundation of this story was built. I would also like to thank Ellen Smith Parker. I know that she spent many hours editing this book and for that I'm grateful. Without her input the book would be incomplete.

To all the others that I've never met that had a hand in editing and offering insightful input, you know who you are, and I thank you. Someday, God Willing I will get to know you.

Lastly, during the process of writing this book from prison, there were many people that witnessed from afar, me transform into a New Man. As I morphed and shed my old skin; the process at times was painful. I want to thank all of you who've continued to email, write, answer my calls, and support me during this season of my life. Your friendships and love have allowed that growth to be bearable. To those family and friends, you've been as much a part in the creation of this book as anyone, and you also know who you are, so "Thank you".

"For by grace you have been saved through faith, and that not of yourselves; it is the gift of God, not of works, lest anyone should boast. For we are His workmanship, created in Christ Jesus for good works, which God prepared beforehand that we should walk in them." (Ephesians 2:8-10)

Cody Lanus

FOREWORD

Meeting Cody Lanus has come from a series of coincidences and also a blessing. I was first introduced and had the opportunity to meet Cody while visiting a friend at Butner Prison Camp. When you hear that God works in mysterious ways, He has proven it here several times over. As you will learn in reading this book, Cody and Gary's meeting was initially confrontational. Through the story of the rose, and many others Cody was able to learn, grow, accept, and understand God's complete love for us-no matter when, where or how. Through a great deal of pushing and pulling, unique circumstances, and undying persistence this story of struggle and reward has come to fruition. I am proud to know Cody and all he has accomplished through the raw emotional telling of his personal demons that he has chosen to share with his readers. Healing emotional wounds that follow us into our adult lives is tough at best. The blessing in all of it is that we **can** make it through. It would be fantastic for many of us to go back and do a makeover to experience the love, approval, and guidance we all crave, and sensed we were lacking. However, if that were to be, we wouldn't have the opportunity of growth through this learning opportunity. This story allows healing and shows where we get that restorative power. Hebrews 11:1 to me says that 'faith is being sure of what we hope for, and certain of what we do not see'. Regardless of your level of faith, or your understanding of it, this book is bound to raise the faith within you.

If you were to go out and search the web or literature for the definition of forgiveness, you would find that it is listed as "the action or process of forgiving or being forgiven--release of debt". The Bible has generously spoken about forgiveness in the sense of who, when and how. It can be made to sound simple enough, but in actuality it is one of the most challenging facets of the human experience. It usually involves recovery from a previous event or trauma, either to us, or possibly caused by us. It is undoubtedly messy and a non-linear process. The physical, emotional and the spiritual are all interwoven, creating a complex pattern of reactions and *of* actions. When, where and how you choose to go on your own journey to find those truths is paramount. You will find that you are able to gain rational forgiveness through validation and reasoning, but true spiritual forgiveness is learned through complete understanding of God and what he did for each of us. It manifests itself in each of us through our acceptance of it, embracing it, and holding it as a foundation of our lives.

Cody has proven to be a gifted writer, who holds the reader's attention through his personal experiences. We too can learn these mechanisms that enable us to attain the freedom of forgiveness. To gain peace and joy in our lives by being tolerant of ourselves and merciful to others as God in Christ has done for all of us. Cody's own story of gain and of loss throughout his younger life and subsequent addictions, whether tattoos, steroids, alcohol, or Fentanyl are told in a manner that is profoundly thoughtful. He is able to show who and what gives us the power and inspiration to forgive ourselves, as well as those who have caused pain and loss in our lives: through the reality of God's love for each and every one of us. Through his own experiences he has taught the readers the true power of how God's love can liberate us. Cody has been able to gain strength from the writing process himself and shared the "antidote" of how we can lessen pain through forgiveness of ourselves and of others and arrive at peace. This is determined by the power of having faith in God's grace: Jesus Christ in our lives, and using that guidance, to discover and live a better life. The demons of distraction cause us to lose our focus on the blessings in life and what we are called to do through the position we hold in Christ. If we make the decision to turn our lives to God, admit we need his path in our life, we *will* win. Christ removed all the chains of bondage so that we could live free, with the blessings of the Spirit in us. Cody made this discovery and now shares it with his readers how they too can be righteous, created in His image and living as a follower of Christ-in spirit, in mind, and in the truth.

When we are able to find this common denominator of faith and of hope and of love that holds us together, we are able to move in the direction of healing and freedom of unresolved pain of the past. The bad memories that hang on in our minds and interfere with life will be released. God tells us to forgive one another because He paid the paramount cost for our sin with His own Son. If we can be the recipients of such great forgiveness, we can learn how to offer that forgiveness to others and ourselves. When we do, we discover that we are the ones who have been set free. Yes, even free from the addictions that stalked Cody for years.

For every part I have had in seeing this move from paper to print, I have been blessed. Blessed with a new friend, a new appreciation for life, and a new ability to find my own healing in the process. I have complete faith as you embark on this journey, either for yourself or someone you hold dear, you too can find the same. Regardless of your level of faith, or your belief in the higher power of God, these stories will have profound impact on your life, and allow you to embrace the benefit of change. Blessings to you as you too move forward.

Ellen Smith Parker 2020

PREFACE

THE SEARCH FOR THE ANTIDOTE

There's a good chance that I know you much better than you realize. I believe this to be true because I believe in both destiny and fate. I believe that nothing is coincidental. For this book to land in your hands is proof of that. The same Higher power that called me to write this book is the same Higher power that called you to receive it. For that reason, we are one and the same. Let me explain.

Look back to the events that led this book to be in your possession. Really take a moment and think on this. Was it given to you by a friend or loved one? Was it pulled from a 'self-help' section you gravitated toward? Did the cover appeal to you? Was it the featured book in a reading group of some kind?

My point is this, all of these factors would make us extremely alike. Why? My summation is this. We are people that are searching relentlessly for happiness. People who would love the life of happiness, free of the pain that seems to be keeping us from having it. In that aspect, let me tell you, we are almost identical. For me, the pain was addiction. By framing it in that way it manifested itself within my life and affected more areas than even I would have imagined.

Through my journey of discovery that you are about to embark on, the framing of my addiction would be turned upside down.

Now, what's occurring today in this country with addiction is absolutely devastating. And because of its grip on America and the havoc it wreaked in my life, I am extremely passionate about helping fight the battle against it. I believe the deep emotions within that passion, in part have given me the unique ability to transcribe my words and thoughts persuasively to paper.

My motivation to write this book came from my eye-opening awareness that nobody should have to experience the pain in the way that I did. The bigger challenge was in accepting that they still do. I wrote this book, this entire book, from a prison cell. I didn't write it thinking of myself as an author because I never felt that I was one, even during the painstakingly beautiful process of writing. My story was revealed to be different in the fact that by writing it I discover the cure to 'my' pain within its very words. I discovered what was necessary to fill what I came to recognize and call 'my' voids.

I wrote this story as a man searching relentlessly for answers to the position, I found myself in, Prison. How did I get myself here? I was well aware of the foolish decisions I made to end up in an 8x10 foot cell, but I felt it ran deeper than just that foolishness. I knew that to truly uncover my pain I'd have to go much deeper than the surface. To a much harder place to process and digest. I'd have to face my demons. Most people never choose to do such a thing. They, like me feel as if they are paralyzed to do so. Their minds cannot fathom seeking out what they see as more pain in order to find pain relief! Therefore, they remain right where I was, painfully stuck in my addiction.

By exposing my journey of discovery in this book, I pray you are able to, in turn discover yourself. Discover what it is that creates and what is necessary to fill your voids. Discover that missing piece of the puzzle that seems to allude us all, no matter how hard on the surface we look for it. The missing piece that, without it, damages relationships, creates the formula for addictions, causes many pains and lays burdens of many kinds. Yet once discovered and applied, all those difficult things in your life have the ability to be corrected, mended, even eradicated.

Because I don't claim to be an author, I don't claim this book to be a perfect piece of prose. However, I believe it to be the absolute truth. A raw voice on a debilitating epidemic that has silently swept our country. Small towns and large cities. African Americans, Caucasians, and Hispanics. In fact, no ethnic community is exempt. Nor the wealthy or poor, young, or old, boys or girls, men, or women. There's a good chance you know someone, if not yourself that is struggling with an addiction that aims to rob them from the happiness they can have.

My intentions are not to offend anyone by 'keeping it real' so if I do, let me apologize in advance. My intentions are however to make a lasting impression on whoever reads this. And a lasting change in the life of those that apply the anecdote that I discovered. Not to create hysteria and make the masses run away in an attempt to change, but to plant a seed. And if that seed is planted, along with a little watering of fresh thought, the rest will take care of itself. I'm certain of that. Why? Because it happened to me. Something you'll soon discover inside these pages.

Most books that are started are never finished, let alone applied. If I can 'reach' you, it won't be because it was like every other book.

It will be because of the emotions it pulled from you. The connection it caused. The actions it moved you to take. The beauty of the person it allowed you to see, you! These things I pray. When they occur in you, I will know another circle has been completed.

The truths within this book have set me free, despite my incarceration. They are now at your fingertips awaiting your call.

You will find I say the words 'God' or 'Jesus' in this book, and I understand those words may be seen and used differently for you. 'Creator' or 'Universe' may resonate better and help you better process what I'm saying, and that's perfectly fine. This isn't a 'Christian' book per se, although it may be found on a 'Christian' bookshelf. This is an 'Everyone allowed to discover 'Self-worth, Happiness and Freedom' book. Most importantly this book is the revelation of my story, letting people see that 'rock bottom' is not a necessary place that has to be reached in order to find actual change for their life. And one does not need to find themselves in prison to receive it either. Or find a loved one, friend, or acquaintance gone at the hand of the pain in order to recognize it. Or be contemplating the same themselves to live anew in it. Yet, if you are any one of these, this book is especially for you. Read on my friend and discover it.

The ideals found in the telling of my story are rooted in all faiths and all religions, not just mine. So, don't let the words 'God' or 'Jesus' deter you from reading the book. To reach the people I intend to reach, I must remain open minded. Something I continue to work on daily. Your beliefs are just as important as mine, despite the different words we may use for the Higher Power. The Power which we believe in and entrust to produce the increase in us for a better life.

By whatever means you find this book has come to be held in your hands, know that its creation was meant for you, yes, YOU! If you're anything like me, which I'm sure you are, you're searching for a way to a pain-free life. Or looking for a genuine path to a pain-free life to offer someone you love and care about. A fearless, courage driven life. A life rooted in Faith, sobriety, and joyful balance. A life we jump out of bed to experience, day in and day out.

The book you now hold will take some application and it will not all be comfortable. Facing voids and pain never is. Yet, I assure you that whatever pain you wish to expel, it CAN and WILL be done.

Happiness is rooted in Love and I believe a major component to that is learning to love yourself. Yes, it is a cliché that has been seemingly worn out with time. But allow yourself to experience its truth within these pages. For, when you don't feel worthy and the negative forces that exist attempt to pull you in, the results can be dramatically 'un-loving'. Especially, when it is personal. So, don't think for a second that the darkness can't consume you. Healing is within reach though, and much easier obtained than you know. Let me show you how. Follow me on my journey of discovery exactly how it played out for me. See if you cannot find yourself or that loved one you are reading this for deep within it.

No matter the purpose of your calling to have this book in your hand, you will be shaped anew by it. Give yourself permission to do just that and embrace your journey within mine.

Together we will embrace the better life.

'Cody'

PROLOGUE

THE RESCUE

They didn't cuff him. They didn't need to. To him, he'd been rescued. Something he saw no need in fleeing from. He didn't need to guess anymore. Death or Prison? He knew which one he'd reached. A Tupac song he'd willed into existence. 'His' existence. For him, you could have put the Federal Agents up there with the Narcan that had previously brought him back to life, Guardian Angels. He didn't want to hurt them he wanted to hug them.

He told the manager at the gym he'd have to cancel the class for the day, "something big came up," he told him. "Life changing as a matter of fact," he continued. He'd probably be gone for longer than a day but "Nobody needed to know that" Cody thought as he walked out the front door of the gym with Federal Agents in front and behind him. Cody climbed into the front seat of a black SUV and began the trek back home to the other side of Omaha with the DEA. The convoy he was part of, the vehicles that had swarmed the gym. He felt famous in a sense. The last time he had police escorts was the National Championship game he played in during college. The very last football game he'd played in. "I wonder what my coaches would think now?" he thought.

Breaking the silence an agent in the back seat spoke up, "Your package has been intercepted."

He deduced immediately it was the order he had placed a few days prior. He knew in his gut what had happened. He didn't want to accept it but definitely he knew. He was certain who it was that had helped the Feds. These were the same black SUVs he had seen a few days earlier roaming around his house. As much as he wanted to ignore the truth he couldn't. He knew his friend had set him up.

"You're facing 20 years in Federal prison for conspiracy to distribute Fentanyl. We expect total honesty from this point forward," the agent continued. The rest of the way to Cody's house they rode in silence. "20 years!" Cody thought sitting in the front seat of the SUV.

The convoy pulled up to Cody's house and was met by a barrage of other vehicles. "Between five and ten" Cody deduced. Men in bulletproof vests with 'DEA' and 'Federal Agent' written in yellow letters on the back of the vests stepped rapidly from all of them. They ran towards Cody's house, rifles in hand. Eyeball to scope. Doing the crouched running that is so often associated with soldiers. They surrounded Cody's house, pointing the guns at windows and doors. They stayed ready, waiting for some sort of signal as if from a man of higher rank. A man with a battering ram approached the front door. Ready to blast it off its hinges. An expense Cody deemed silently, "Ridiculous!". Doing what he thought sensible at that very moment, Cody reached into his pocket and fished for his keys. Within a microsecond he was stopped by the sound of a hammer being cocked behind him. Cody froze, knew what the sound meant. "They're keys to the front door," Cody said. "Pull them out slowly," the agent replied. Cody did as he was told. Slowly holding the keys at shoulder length and jingling them. "You can just unlock the door. Nobody is inside. No need to mess my door up," Cody continued.

They took the keys from Cody and stormed in like Navy Seals as he watched from the black SUV, the agent still behind him. All Cody could think about as they raided his house was getting a fix, a shot. He wasn't thinking about the agents inside or the one sitting behind him with the gun. All he could think about was getting high. Anything would suffice: Fentanyl, Percocet, OxyContin, Vicodin- even Hydrocodone would do the trick. He'd take whatever he could get. The first bead of the sweat of withdrawal moved its way down Cody's face. He was sure that the Fed's intervention wouldn't in- volve a tapering off of opiates. "This won't be comfortable," Cody thought. Her grip, strong. Her roots, deep. Addiction.

A man in fatigues appeared at the front door. "Probably some sort of ex-military," Cody thought. He waved Cody and the agent behind him to get inside the house. This time Cody wouldn't make any sudden movements. He let the agent open his door.

Now inside Cody sat at his kitchen table with multiple Federal Agents asking a barrage of questions. Simple questions at first like why and how he got involved with Fentanyl to more complicated ones involving Cody's importing methods. "Let's get something straight," the head agent in charge said, "Aside from finding Jimmy Hoffa in your basement you'll be free on pre-trial release," He then went into detail about this thing he kept referring to as 'pre-trial release'. It appeared as a surprise to Cody, with his clean criminal history, he would be free to continue his life prior to a trial. Aside from drug selling and use, if he were able to fulfill the requirements of the pre-trial release, he would remain free. Clean urine, Cody was informed, would also be one of these stipulations. Cody was glad he would remain free, but then again, he kind of wished he wouldn't. What was swirling in his head on this news was "Could I maintain?"

Cody knew he had to be at work at his law-abiding job in a few hours. He wanted them to finish their search and leave. They already had boxes full of steroids and steroid making equipment. All the things Cody and Jason had initially invested in to get the business going. Now, all being carried out in boxes by the Feds. "We need to bring you down to headquarters and get you processed in." an agent informed him. "Great," Cody thought "Another trip across Omaha with the agent behind me!" So, back to the black SUV they went.

The DEA headquarters was literally a block from Jason's house. You could have practically thrown a stone out of Jason's front door and hit their building; it was that close. "How Ironic," Cody thought with all the times they were dealing right there.

Once inside headquarters, the Feds did their thing. Fingerprints and paperwork that now identified Cody as some sort of soon to be 'inmate' or 'felon' of some kind. Cody wasn't sure which, "Probably both." he guessed.

With that part over Cody was left in a tiny holding cell waiting for the next phase to begin. "Whatever that may be," Cody thought. A couple of detainees next to him in the cell were yelling something in Spanish. "They must be having as good of a day as me," Cody said to himself. Sitting there he couldn't help but have his mind think about the impact of all this on his work. "What are my bosses going to think if they find out?" he thought. "I'll need to take a week of vacation; these next few days will be rough." Knowing the pain of the withdraws he was about to endure. The ones that were nipping at him already as he sat in the cell inside the DEA headquarters.

Thirty minutes later the cell door opened. An agent with a camera in his hand stood in the doorway. "We need to get a picture of all your tattoos," he said. "Tattoos?" Cody thought while standing and smiling as he pulled the shirt over his head giving the agent the first glimpse of his tattoo covered torso and sides. Cody stood still, waiting for the agent's instructions. "Got any on your back?" the agent asked. He didn't need to say anything, Cody just turned. The 'Tribal Sun' on his shoulder blade and the Chinese symbols on each arm were easily visible for the agent to photograph. Snap. Cody saw the flash on the wall in front of him. A non-verbal queue that the picture had been taken. As he turned back around the agent asked, "What do those symbols mean?" Not seeming to need any formal answer, as he didn't have pen or paper, Cody deduced he was asking out of his own curiosity. Being a question Cody was by now used to answering he responded, "Faith and Courage,". "Well you're going to need a whole lot of both of those in the upcoming months." the agent seemed to joke. Now bringing the camera up to his face again. A face that resembled most of the other agents. Square Jaw. Neat hair. Ex-military. A face Cody thought he had seen before at one of the gyms he frequented. A face he probably 'had' seen at that very gym. "A cops face," Cody thought. The agent continued snapping close up pictures of Cody's chest and torso, the skulls in their various forms. When the agent went to photograph Cody's side, he naturally picked his arms up, resting his hands on his head. The girl tattoo was first. The agent this time getting close like a professional photographer. Snap. Snap. Cody felt like a piece of artwork. The agent next moved to the other side, to the 'Thug-Life' tattoo. He stopped for a second then raised the camera to his face asking as if perplexed through a laugh, "Why the fuck would you ever put that on your body?" Snap. Snap. The flash once again bouncing off the small concrete walls in the tiny cell with its stainless-steel toilet.

Just then, Cody was beginning to feel dizzy. He wanted to get out of there. He was defeated. He was tired. He was soon to be indicted. While still thinking on how he should respond to the agents "Thug-Life" question he heard himself blurt out the only thing that seemed to come. "It's a long story."

1

THE SPIRALING

...INWARD

Look at this moron! He had the brains to know you are not supposed to seduce your clients, let alone smoke 'weed' with them. Yet it appears that is exactly what was happening. He knew full well the two most important unwritten rules of a successful male Fitness Trainer of women. They seemed simple enough and pretty straight forward.

Rule #1 If you want to continue getting paid, never, ever, never, ever let your mind wander into getting 'cozy' with the Trainee! Keep the relationship strictly professional.

Rule #2 To help assure compliance with Rule #1, never, ever, never, ever go to their home, or invite them to yours!

He knew through experience that breaking these two rules never ended well and always resulted in at least one less client, which ultimately meant at least one less paycheck. He also knew that a woman's willingness to achieve 'personal physical fitness' never stood up against the awkwardness of a 'one-night stand' with her trainer. Yet, weighing these rules and his options over time he decided he would be able to bend them to his will.

He was thinking back on this very decision as he took another 'toke' of the 'weed-filled' blunt that his pretty trainee just passed him while drawing closer to her strictly for 'warmth'. So, he smiled as he sat on her tiny balcony looking over the parking lot at the other college students milling around. He was working through the fog of smoke and hormones to remember if any part of the 'rules' technically forbids him from 'getting high' with a trainee!? His conclusion, "At this very moment if there are any such restricting parts of the rules, 'rules' be damned!"

By this time, they had already spent some significant personal time together. A few months actually. Not only was he her 'rules breaking' personal fitness trainer, but he was now her coworker at the Clarinda Academy, a juvenile placement facility in the next town over. This is where he found himself pushing the boundaries of potentially more serious rules. He was a full-time Floor Supervisor of youth counselors. She was a youth counselor, working as an intern while finishing her psychology degree at Northwest Missouri State. Yet, they worked on different floors. So, with that logistics at play, he figured he technically 'wasn't' her boss therefore, the rules of fraternizing wouldn't apply to them. At least that was the 'mantra' he let roll through his mind as they began to kiss on the balcony. The same 'mantra' that was working so well for him as her personal 'Trainer'!

He knew this would eventually happen, or at least deep down he hoped so. Who wouldn't? She was a 21-year-old in her senior year on the accelerated graduation program. Filling summers with class loads and the remaining semesters with 17 credit hours, she had dreams and ambitions. None of which involved sticking around that sleepy Missouri college town. It had nothing to offer her and the quicker she left with her degree in hand the quicker she could begin the next chapter of her life. He sensed she wanted to change the world in some capacity. He could feel it in the energy she emitted. He, on the other hand, had filled his summers with the railing of nights long forgotten and reliving college football memories. Looking backward so to speak, while she was looking forward. He felt as if he had pulled off graduation at 25 by eking out an internship at a local gym. His degree, unlike hers, didn't feel like it required near the same brainpower. He never needed to put forth the hours dedicated to research and other studious endeavors, as she did.

Most football guys, which he was the epitome of, more likely than not, committed themselves to the elementary degrees so they could play ball and not worry about 20-page papers. He had been no different. The four-hour practices were grueling enough, so he never understood how athletes that took real courses ever did it. Secretly he envied them. He remembered being defined once by certain people as a "student-athlete", but "just barely". Thus, taking it as an implication that he wasn't a bonified student or graduate. Now, since college graduation he found himself to be neither. He walked away with a degree in 'Exercise Science' and a piece of paper that seemed to only say he had attended college and completed the classes but nothing significant to brag about. He had no internal or external drive to leave Northwest Missouri State. Now 26 and a year since he graduated, he asked himself, "Why leave?" He was making decent money and was getting busier and busier at the gym, the very gym where he'd met Lauren. She had stumbled in like a damsel in distress so being the suave trainer that he was he quickly took her under his wing, at a discounted rate of course. He began training her for a 'spring break' vacation that she, like thousands of other college kids, would be going on. Cody, not being able to afford them in college had never been on one. In reality, the spring training for football had consumed most of his 'spring break' time anyway.

By this time, his closest friends were off getting married but here he found himself still in Missouri's Northwest College territory. "Oh well!" he thought. So, when Cody met girls like Lauren, he let the encounters solidify his decision to "stick around". The fact that he was not meeting any of the status-quo expectations to move, marry, and or seek the job security like his friends left him feeling a bit washed up though. But for now, he would accept it.

 Like many college kids that hooked up, Cody and Lauren also came from separate walks of life. Yet, even with that they soon became united through fitness, marijuana, and lust. This sort of thing had been going on for years in college towns all over the world so, "Why should it stop with us?" he thought. She was gorgeous and smart and could seemingly have any man she wanted. A thin, dark-haired Italian girl with a great sense of humor. He pondered privately his fortune as he passed her the blunt, "How did I land this one?" This came from the fact that he never had high self-esteem, at least inwardly. Maybe that's one of the reasons he fell in love with the weights and building muscle. He knew it was a bit of a mask he could hide behind, a suit of armor of sorts. "Nobody gave a shit about Clark Kent. " he deduced. "They just wanted Superman."

Finishing the blunt they pulled away from each other and she threw the roach over the balcony to collect with the others. As she turned to go back into the apartment, he caught a glimpse of her backside. She opened the sliding door and stepped inside as his mind began to wander. She had a TV in the living room, but he hadn't seen her as the TV type of girl. She had never watched it in the few times he'd been over or even mentioned it. She was to him more of the conversational type. More of the 21 questions type. They took a seat on the couch and began chatting away. Making conversation through random bursts from their weed-mind laughter.

Cody believed they had become attracted to each other by their love for the spontaneity of life and their willingness to live it. They both certainly liked how the other looked but that was just an added bonus. It was really the weekly monotonous training sessions, powered up by her effervescent personality and his hand in cultivating it that created the chemistry between them. He would like to think that he had chosen women based on their compatibility but at least with the ones before Lauren, it had seemed more like how they might perform in bed.

He felt internally nervous with Lauren despite putting on a decent show of brawn. "When in doubt be dominant in any way possible. Brag about yourself or at least flex something. Or both." he always told himself. Yet, he sensed he was being a bit idiotic now. "She isn't like the others. She doesn't care how macho I am" he told himself. For the first time despite those attempts at brawn, she somehow made him feel a bit submissive. A feeling he was beginning to sense he liked. A bit of a role reversal for sure. "How does this petite girl with the world ahead of her enjoy my company?" He had now seen her in her personal and professional life enough to know she was becoming an Italian goddess of sorts to him. He, on the other hand, felt himself a 'gypsy soul' of sorts. As if waiting for someone or something to carry him out of this town, not being capable yet to do it on his own. "Was this the one?" he mused.

He realized that her internship would be finished soon, and it was pretty likely that another Midwest City would be calling her away. Away from him, back to her family, friends, and higher education's rewards. His bet was that her life wouldn't stop at a bachelor's degree. Not with her expressed ambitions to be a child psychiatrist. Then again, how was he to know such things?

Cody, in his mind, wasn't even supposed to make it this far with Fitness Training and Youth Counseling success, let alone in a relationship with a girl the likes of Lauren. Six years ago, he felt as if a few back in his hometown would have held out high hopes that he would even obtain a degree. Back then as a senior in high school, he knew he had neglected class work by earning credits through a vocational program building homes and not what others would call serious academic learning. "So, without really testing his aptitude to get through basic classwork back then how would he possibly survive at the college level?" was what he sensed most thought of him. They knew him only as one to succeed on the physical field of competition and not on the field of academics. He had left them and headed off to Northwest hoping they were wrong and praying that his football prowess would continue to cover him until he learned new ways to achieve at the college level.

Coming out of the daydream of his life, he found himself still sitting there smiling at Lauren. Then, to his amazement, they began talking about the future and what it held for them individually. What was next on the horizon? Right in the middle of him trying to sound intelligent, confident, and convincing in what he felt was a bunch of rambling hope, she grabbed his hand, and her demeanor became really serious, and she stared straight in his eyes. Her body language changed, and her dark eyes widened. He set staring back as if paralyzed. Wiping her dark hair from her slender face Lauren spoke something he'd never forget, something that would change the course of his life, "*Cody, you should come to Omaha with me!*"

...OUTWARD

His 'bread & butter' was personal training. If he could do anything, he could do that. Help people reach fitness goals seemed to come naturally. He had an impressive resume to prove it. It came from his training the elderly and youth and helping with Special Olympics. He had worked with every fitness demographic through college. Also, he had helped run several New Year's Challenge weight loss programs for the community at Northwest. Through college athletics he knew he was able to push his physical limitations to great levels. He also knew he was darn good at transferring that knowledge into pushing and motivating the actions of everyday people that had a heart of desire. At the Community Center where he had met Lauren, he had helped people obtain their sought-after physiques. From the gym to the basketball courts, to the cardio rooms, Cody utilized the entire space of the facility to train his clients. Even a few 'lunges' in the parking lot were a possibility.

With that resume and knowledge, he was able to land a training gig at a local '24 Hour Fitness' close to their new Omaha apartment. It was a corporate gym that drained him of 50% of his hourly rate, so it wasn't part of his permanent plan, but it was a beginning. Something to pay the bills while they waited for their training classes to start. What they saw as their real jobs, made possible by their time working as Youth Counselors back at Clarinda Academy.

'Behavioral Health Technicians' they would soon be, at a local youth facility. 'The' local youth facility to be exact. It was so large and renowned it had become a 'Town' within Omaha. The infamous 'Boys Town'. A behemoth facility that housed their youth in real homes. It had its own High School and even a Police and Fire station along with its own Church. Because it was a Catholic organization, going to church and prayers before meals would be mandatory for both of them. They would participate in these daily prayers and worship service (Mass) more out of compliance with work than out of their personal choices. They would seemingly master the act of an outward 'Christian' appearance. Outside of that, he didn't personally pray alone and only read the bible when the opportunity arrived at work. Together, their spiritual faith rarely extended out of the workplace. They would not find themselves praying together in their personal lives and rarely discussed it. And attending church outside of Boys Town was only a yearly holiday event respected only to fulfill what they saw as Lauren's family obligation.

Millions of dollars were funneled into Boys Town by devout Catholics and others all over the United States. It was 'The' youth facility of all youth facilities in America. Cody and Lauren began to speak of plans to become teaching parents within it; a married couple that lives in one of the homes with the kids and acting like their parents. All to establish a family setting. Boys Town prided itself on raising kids in real family atmospheres and believed this was the key to all correct youth development. But until that developed, they would first need to find jobs for a few months, so they applied.

Training seemed the only way to bridge that gap. Other than the money, her need to be inseparable from Cody was the reason she applied at the same gym along with him. She harbored a touch of jealousy and preferred to be around when he trained other women. He deduced she was not lost to the memory of how they became a couple. Through training, she knew how they had fallen in love and was not comfortable with him continuing the occupation. At least not alone! Having discussed it they compromised by deciding to work together. "Why not?" he thought. "We're going to be working together at Boys Town." He really didn't mind though. He found it was cute that she seemed so obsessed with him. He never had that before and in a weird way, he liked it. He no longer felt submissive in her presence but instead empowered. This is what he saw that really made her inseparable from him.

She immediately landed the front desk job greeting people and answering phones. They would be a real package deal as he began training new clients. Both would be eyeing each other in between sets. Smiling and making faces at each other, they became ridiculous. But it seemed all good as they were poised to conquer the world together, so it seemed. It wasn't long before the redundancy, complacency, intimacy, and communication of the relationship became what most relationships seem to eventually become, work. The conquering of the world became lost in the motion of their two-job life cycle. As with many Millennials and the many young generations that came before them, they had no clue what to do during this phase of life. Cody and Lauren fell right in line with so many others. The novelties wore off and sex stopped fixing their problems. They needed a backup plan, but they did not have one and seemed to slowly lose the energy to try and find one. Of course, the catalyst to most of their arguments was the fact that they were broke. They were in a new expensive city with high expectations trying to impress people they didn't really care about. They seemed stuck. This was not proving to be a good thing in their floundering relationship. Keeping up with the Jones' had never appealed to him yet for some reason he found himself living with Lauren in a sprawling condo in the expensive west side of Omaha. The pool came along with several other amenities and an inflated rent. The reason for him to accept it was simple. She wanted it, so he agreed to 'make it happen'. But soon his funds were running out and the arguments began to have a direct correlation with the increasingly low single-digit balances in his accounts. Soon his bravado kicked in, "If money was the issue, then the money is what I'd get". He began telling himself. His pride was too precious to lose any of this.

Downgrades and parent loans didn't exist to him. He put himself through college asking for minimal help from his parents. They had divorced when he was young, and times had been tough growing up with a mother being so young herself. He knew that through hard work, she had graduated from college despite having three kids. She always found ways to make ends meet and provide a substantial life, no matter what obstacles were ahead of her. His mother was tough, and he repeatedly told himself, "If she can do it, so can I." Then his mind doubled down on its determination as he thought about Lauren's parents. "What would they think of me if I couldn't provide for their daughter?" the questions began. "Am I really capable of taking care of her?" they continued.

Then it came. One day while contemplating his fate and searching for some resolution he remembered it. He remembered that which he had planned to leave back in Missouri and with his Northwest college days forever. He remembered how he had made money in a previous pinch and how he had made it fast. "Can I salvage this relationship?" he really began to ask himself.

The question of what price would he be willing to pay to save them and personally save face seemed to not leave him alone. "You succeeded at Northwest; can you succeed in Omaha?" he asked himself As he drove to the gym one morning the wheels began to turn, not on his car but in his mind. The wheels of his past began to be re-created into possibilities of the future. The criminal mind and its capability, the one he had planned to leave behind, hoping he'd never have to uncover it again began spinning, seemingly at its own will. He came upon a bumper sticker that read 'WWJD', "What 'would' Jesus do?" He wondered not what Jesus would do but what he would have to do if he chose this path. But to make it fit within the confines of the bumper sticker and to appease his mind he deduced, "As long as Lauren doesn't find out, it isn't wrong, is it? Jesus would do what Jesus had to do to survive, wouldn't he?" He smiled as he pulled up to the gym feeling a possibility of renewed hope.

The lies in his head had begun to resurface. During his previous life in college athletics while building muscle and training clients he had quickly found how beneficial steroids could be. He witnessed their popularity amongst not only serious athletes but recreational gymgoers as well. Building, Training, and Steroids seemed to go hand in hand, at least in the circle he lived. One didn't seem to exist without the other. Whether it was for his personal use or at the request of clients and athletes, he quickly discovered a financial opportunity in their high demand. Through several friends and much research, he found out the process of obtaining the steroids needed. It seemed to Cody that any willing person with a computer could access the thousands of underground websites that readily sold them. All with the click of a mouse. He wasn't sure why they all came from overseas, but he did wonder "If so, many other countries allowed them, why didn't the U.S?" Continuing his convincing rationale, "They don't get you high. People don't rob people for them. People don't need them like some people need crack." That's all it seemed to take for him to make a lucrative run at being a profitable middleman during college. Though he had quit selling steroids when he left, he still regularly used them, unbeknown to Lauren.

He realized now that he didn't know anybody in Omaha in that arena and he had left all his buyers in college. He remembered that he had clearly convinced himself that he was helping friends obtain their fitness goals. "I wasn't a drug dealer," he told himself any time the notion of it being wrong tried to enter his mind. "Drug dealers sell hard drugs" he would continue. It seemed that he was ripe to begin repeating and believing those same statements.

Now that he was in Omaha, he realized he didn't have those friends to supply anymore. Reconnecting with them and mailing steroids would be too risky. He continued to accept the fact that he was receiving them personally, but the thought of sending them out seemed too scary for him. At some point, he thought to himself "When was the last time I went a week without an injection? It sure has been a while. Maybe I should just take a break from this whole thing?" Then another voice jumped in, "Then again, maybe not!".

It was surprising to him that this desire for assistance all started with over-the-counter supplements at his local GNC. The prohormones that mimic testosterone were considered the 'good stuff' back then. This all started in the 8th grade when his body dysmorphia started. He didn't see his daily obsession with trying to fix perceived flaws in his muscular appearance as a problem. Yet, he knew that what others would see in him, he seemed never to see in himself. It was as if he had a reverse condition of anorexia where the muscle he had was never enough. So, then to go for a little chemical assistance seemed quite natural. Since College, when the GNC's 'good stuff' wasn't enough he went on to obtain the 'real stuff', steroids from overseas via a few 'clicks' on his computer. Though the needles didn't come with the orders, buying them was just as easy. Click. Add. Click. Buy. Click. Send. A few days later some packages delivered by the mailman solidified his abilities. He couldn't inject himself at first. He couldn't muster the courage needed to penetrate the long thin piece of metal into his skin. He was terrified of needles and had to have the assistance of a friend from his 'steroid using circle' show him the way. Over time he learned to do it himself. He had come a long way from swallowing the prohormones. He could even load and inject in the car as he often had to do to avoid being caught by Lauren.

For those friends who hadn't known what sites to use or were too scared to access them, they had no worries. Cody would do it for them, at an inflated price of course. He had soon become the middleman between buyer and source via the internet. It was game on, business on.

All that was supposed to be left back at college, in his past, where he had intended to leave it. Or so he thought.

...DOWNWARD

Cody remembered learning that behind every guy shooting testosterone into his delts and ass was another guy getting it for him off the internet. He had been both of those guys in college. "Why couldn't

I be that same guy in a city like Omaha? I can support my personal use and fix all my relationship issues with a few clicks a week" he started thinking. "Of course, I'd have to expand the lie, and tell Lauren the new packages were something else. Better yet, I can get a PO Box. One of the big ones that accepted all package sizes."

"It's all starting to feel like a plan, but I will need help getting started. I will need a small client base that could trust me," he continued formulating. "I think I know just the guy to talk to", a voice now seeming to convince him to act. A new voice. A voice he hadn't remembered hearing before or hadn't heard from in his head for a long time. Not his, but hers. A persistent voice pushing to do what he knew he shouldn't. She seemed to be telling him who the very person was that he needed that help from.

Cody knew she picked the right guy to approach when his fellow trainer Jason didn't run in fear when he told him of the steroid business plan. Instead, they soon became friends. They were now bonding through the love of training and taking steroids. They rapidly began sharing each other's training clients, their sites, and their buyers. The partnership they formed amplified their pocketbooks, growing their illegal business into something quite profitable in a short period of time. Jason was a genius with a computer. He knew the best sites. The cheapest and quickest. Cody was a genius with the people and the delivery. They were so successful in fact within one year of providing steroids to the market in Omaha, they had cornered it. He was the mouthpiece and Jason the man behind the ordering. Together they felt like they were an unstoppable force.

Cody's lifestyle was rapidly changing. He started to live life in the fast lane and to him, Lauren couldn't keep up. Lauren had quit Boys

Town while Cody had stayed on. Their occupation, the only stabilizing factor in their crumbling relationship was now gone. They only saw each other at night, late at night. Most of the time Cody would come in the door to see Lauren fast asleep. Her long dark hair resting on the pillow, the woman he used to chase. The time they spent together at night had been replaced with making steroids. Cody was now chasing a new obsession. Cody was tired of lying to her. Tired of telling her that "Work ran late." yet again. But he chose to frame it as if she were weighing him down. The temptations for him that came with a life of selling steroids became too much for him to handle within his relationship with her. Having multiple clients meant much more than simply dropping off steroids. The connections were made at night and usually wherever the buyer was at the time. It meant parties and women, money, and status. Those nights provided more stimuli for him than nights coming home to Lauren. He became more infatuated by this 'new existence', this 'new identity' that steroids brought into his life and less and less infatuated with her. The attention he gained 'out and about town' hadn't been felt since leaving the superstar status of the gridiron at college. He now felt he had a life of opportunities he saw quickly approaching him.

"Set sail with Lauren or jump ship and embrace this 'new life' fully," he thought as he sat one evening in a strip club sipping Grey Goose. As much as he wanted a life with Lauren, it terrified him just as much. "Nobody can cage me," he defensively thought. He had so many new friends that were having the times of their lives. Single. Rich. Definitely not monogamous. "Leave Lauren." The voice continually told him. The things he told himself time and time again to avoid, he did not. He slowly began to succumb to the voice, finally cheating on Lauren. He knew it was time to move on. Then, one day it was over.

He packed his bags and told Lauren goodbye. She cried and cried and begged him to stay. He just got in his car and sped away. Out of her life. He had actually jumped ship. He realized that money hadn't solved their problems. It had amplified them and now Lauren was gone. He convinced himself he didn't need her. He didn't need anyone. Except, of course, Jason. They became so successful they quit working at the gym. They didn't need it, especially after the money started coming in. All they felt they needed from the gym now was a base of buyers and when that was obtained the gym jobs seemed unnecessary. "Now our base of clients has been established, word of mouth will do the rest," he thought. And it did. He remained working at Boys Town mainly for the insurance. Through all this, even amazing to himself, was the fact that by day he was helping those kids, only to then go out and illegally sell steroids to adults by night. He knew he was living a double life. A life that nobody seemed to suspect. A Jekyll and Hyde life. More deplorable than he let himself believe, for he knew deep down that he would, if exposed be seen as a monster in disguise. A youth care supervisor and a money-making drug user/supplier all in one. Preaching morals during the day and making drop-offs at night. He knew it was a messed-up way to live but seemed powerless to change it or even to want to change it. He was working overtime to keep it all 'Ok' in his head.

His faith seemed to consist of mandatory praying every day at work with Father Peter, one of the head priests of Boys Town. A 'man of God' like Father Peter was in a long line of priests who had held that position ever since its existence with the first Father Flannigan almost a hundred years earlier. One Sunday as he uttered an "Our Father" prayer surrounded by children; Cody began to cry. Not hysterically at first but tears began to flow slowly from in the corners of his sleepy eyes. The night before had been a busy one and it was lingering with him. He decided to get up in the middle of prayer ignoring the several eyes glancing in his direction. He felt he had to get out of there before someone saw him. He went into his office and locked the door. With his head buried in his hands, he sobbed uncontrollably. "My life is a mess and I know it" whispering to himself. As he pulled his head from his hands through teary eyes, he saw the calendar across his office, a picture of Jesus wearing a crown of thorns. He met Jesus' eyes and for a moment they stared at each other. It was that famous picture of Jesus, wearing the crown of thorns, a head tilted and a desperate look on his face. He could only imagine the pain Jesus felt. But as they locked eyes he felt as if the pain wasn't from dragging the cross. He was now certain the pain was from the demon 'Cody' that Jesus saw staring back at him. Cody! He forced himself to push the feeling aside and gathered himself and went back to the circle of prayer. He rejoined Father Peter to finish another day of pretending. Pretending to be someone he wasn't.

With not even a fleeting thought of the epiphany within the Boys Town prayer meeting Cody found himself engaging Jason, "Why are we buying steroids already bottled and labeled when we can do all that ourselves for, I'm sure a fraction of the cost?" So, they decided to calculate the costs together that night as they vaped THC. (No more blunts, weed was now futurized, technologically advanced. They were getting that from the internet too.) "Labels, two types of alcohol, vials, tops, a crimper, some beakers, a filtration system, and some raw powder. That's it, that's all we need to turn a good thing great." Jason was now speaking high on the idea. Of course, he knew some reliable websites they could get everything they needed at the lowest cost possible. Instead of importing a finished product they could import the raw product and finish it themselves. There was even an 'app' they could download that would give them all the correct measurements and amounts for how many bottles they wanted to make. Cody spoke assuredly, "Ok, we'll make it ourselves. Instead of $60-100 a bottle we'll make it for $5, the difference per bottle would be our much higher profit. With the money we've made selling finished bottles the start-up cost would be feasible, about $2,500 each. We have mastered importing them through customs. Raw powder couldn't be much different." they convinced themselves. They were about to go from middlemen to manufacturers. "Ok," he thought, "If possession is 12 months how much extra time comes with manufacturing and trafficking?" Without a hitch came the only convincing answer, "No need to even look, it can't be that much more!". So, he dropped it. He was long past doubting the voice in his head that was telling him "This is a good plan, a good life."

Soon they were off and running and profiting big time. It wasn't long before they expanded out of Omaha, shipping steroids all over the country. Word of mouth had indeed worked and would continue to. They couldn't handle the growing demand. They had quickly become what Cody once searched out, someone to supply steroids strictly for his personal use in college. A good, reliable, trusted source. How the tables had turned.

It had been a couple of years since he'd left Lauren and a year since he'd been 'manufacturing' steroids with Jason. The overseas supplier became quite comfortable with their partnership, or so it seemed by the way they showed it. To their surprise one month the suppliers had thrown in, for the first time, some drugs other than steroids. Free samples it seemed. A little bit of this and a little bit of that and a whole lot of things they hadn't been interested in or would consider touching let alone selling. That is until one night when a 'new high' showed up.

The supplier 'knowledgeably ' had bragged that the fentanyl wasn't even illegal in the U.S., a gray area the DEA wasn't hip to yet, claiming that Synthetics that mimic the real thing were undetectable. So, without much pushback, they accepted that rationale and decided to begin with some personal experimenting. Cody certainly did not know at the time when it happened, that he would never be able to forget, for as long as he lived the euphoric feeling that came with it. The feeling of that amazing 'new high' that first night he snorted fentanyl at Jason's kitchen table. The very place where they'd pretty much committed to making only steroids every evening for the last year. And only getting high vaping THC while they worked. But, on this night the feeling of the Fentanyl circulated through his veins, surging through his blood, powerfully moved him. He sat there and closed his eyes as the drug engulfed him. He thought immediately, in full images, as if happening all together those great days in high school and college playing football, the National Championships, the college memories, the degree, the Italian girl, the sweet innocence he once possessed. He was being possessed by a euphoric game film of his life. By something incredibly different and incredibly powerful. A completely 'new high'. That night a new phase of his life was born.

Snorting it together was amazing. It catapulted them into a super-human two-man team of steroid manufacturers. They ended the night barely able to walk but somehow drove a few miles to the nearest Post Office. Using the kiosk in the middle of the night to ship off the numerous packages. This process soon became a nightly ritual. Yet, it wouldn't be long before they graduated from snorting to shooting fentanyl. All in hopes of a 'higher high'! It was as simple as using the same needles as those they purchased for the steroids. And with this new level of use, something became less and less important. He still had not allowed himself to spend any mind time on the possibility that his life was on an unsustainable trajectory. The fear of letting himself hear the words of the inevitable outcome of such a path kept it just out of earshot. "Two exits. Prison or Death!"

One evening Jason for some reason seemed eager to sport his brand-new ink. As he did and Cody watched, feelings from the past resurfaced immediately. Feelings from a time when he wasn't as dangerous to himself as he had now become. In that moment Cody recognized something. That he would up the ante yet again. That same voice he began to recognize was also telling him something else; get more tattoos, lots of them. "What was this new ambition"?" Cody thought as he watched Jason show off his gleaming new ink. He hadn't thought about getting a new tattoo for a long time. Not since the last one back in college. Not since back when the flashing "Tattoo" sign outside the bar he bounced at caught his attention. Back when getting his tattoos seemed to be a much more risk-taking behavior than it was that night. "I wonder if I can find an artist that will let me get high in the shop?" he thought to himself. More and more things in his life seemed to involve the 'get high' factor as a question.

Not long after Jason's exposition and the tugging, Cody obtained an artist's number from a steroid buyer that was covered from head to toe in 'ink'. No visible free space existed on him unless you wanted to explore areas the sun didn't hit. It had not been that hard to find such a guy from one of the six gyms he frequented and supplied.

Cody's tattoos seemed good enough to him up to that point but when the urge to get inked re-emerged that night at Jason's, talent wasn't a priority prerequisite of the artist. Cody wasn't the newbie entering a Tattoo Shop anymore. He knew it would be a whole new experience from the first time with his high school buddies. He was now an addict, drug user, drug dealer, womanizer, and a maniac.

Cody was still justifying all of this behavior with his meaningful, 'give back' day job working with all those lost kids at Boys Town. This made his drug practice seem a justifiable activity for all the 'good' he was doing there. He was one of those types of addicts that was the hardest of workers and dedicated himself tirelessly to his 'legitimate' trade. A so called 'functioning addict'. He felt his bullshit degree really didn't matter anymore because he now had several postgraduate level and pre-med students working under him. He knew he had become a master of de-escalation and deception techniques. He could easily get the kids and staff to meet his demands and his commands. From the most extreme cases of youth misbehavior, he had become a professional at de-escalation, through words. Words he frequently used on himself to keep the demons at bay who lived just far enough below the surface to make sanity a question and insanity a probability. Yes, he had everything under control, or so he kept telling himself, or so someone kept telling him.

...TOO MUCH

Then it happened. It was during a 'one on one' truthful personal talk session with himself in his car. This was a time when he could think and collect his thoughts. It was during one of these times he reached a point that he realized he was spiraling downhill faster than he could re-correct himself. It was scaring him. Cody's thoughts of a purer life only existed within the hours spent behind a steering wheel. These car talks he'd frequently have with himself and God while driving were the only real words with substance and truth he was having in his life. The lies had become things he now seemed accustomed to. Yet he would often find himself saying "Jesus give me the strength to quit, help me find a way out of this chaos." Then he'd reach his destination, step out of the vehicle and it was like the talks had never happened. Like a switch had been flipped. Stepping into the very environment he had just prayed to get out of. In closing the car door to his 'church', his 'one on one' session with God were over. "If I could only put to action the life I pray to have while driving in my car," he thought many times as he walked on. The reality of his spiraling downhill also moved back into the lie that made it possible to live.

A pre-requisite Cody's new tattoo artist now had to possess was to love drugs as much as him. He wouldn't waste paying cash for this crap. His questions needing answered were "Will the artist let me get high? Will the artist get high? Will the artist let me pay him with a high?" It shouldn't be hard to please the guy as by now Cody was dabbling in everything. MDMA aka 'Molly' as it is referred to on the streets. A popular party drug now being popularized in several rap songs. This along with Benzos, Oxy, Percocet and various other opiates. Though it had all started with steroids, when the supplier started sending samples of this and that, it quickly escalated too much, much more. He had recently ordered a pill press for a grand and had it shipped to his front door. Apparently raw powders existed in every drug, not just steroids. They could pill anything, and they did.

It seemed now that every morning Cody drove to work hung-over from another drug-induced stupor. There were even nights he convinced himself in the car, that certain things hadn't gone awry during the evening, just so he could step in the doors to work with the kids. He felt to think otherwise or to do otherwise would destroy him.

Cody had made a mental note when the guy from the gym covered in tattoos made the comment that his tattoo artist liked opiates. With an internal nod he said, " Yes, a fellow opiate lover". So, with a pocket packed full of opiates in their various forms, he pulled up to the shop. Half-lit up himself his mind was hoping to continue his previous skull collage he'd started in college. As he pulled up to the Tattoo shop across town, strangely located on the upper floor of a convenient store. From the moment he opened the door he realized the shop was insane, the creepiest one he'd ever seen. The front desk was a real coffin and the artist Kevin had horror movie memorabilia scattered around the room, packed into every corner. The walls were covered too. Freddy Krueger autographed posters, an authentic hand from the movie, a Jason hockey mask, a machete covered in blood. It was like walking into a haunted house on Halloween.

"This guy must be obsessed, possibly possessed", Cody thought as he looked around mesmerized. This shop was a demonic rat's nest. The Nightmare wasn't on Elm Street, it was right here in this shop. It lived in this guy's head. "Cool", Cody strangely thought. "This is going to be interesting".

Through a few pre-meeting texts they had communicated more in regard to the recreational drug use they'd partake in and not really any details about the actual tattooing itself. "What kind of stuff you got?" Kevin had asked. "Oh, you know, a little bit of this a little bit of that", he had cautiously replied via text. So, once they introduced themselves and before any talk of tattooing began, they both knew intuitively what mattered most. Cody pulled the bag of Oxy pills from his pocket and the artist quickly grabbed the ceramic skull that was lying on the coffin top décor in order to crush them into powder. Kevin wasn't messing around. A credit card here, a rolled twenty there; the room was quickly filled with the sound of snorting drugs. No words, just the sniffling of powder being manually lifted from the surface of the coffin countertop to the bloodstream via nostrils. Cody knew right then he had Kevin in the palm of his hand. From this point forward paying for tattoos would be free, "Well, for the most part anyway" he thought to himself.

Getting tattoos had now infiltrated his circle. His group of drugs using friends. Not only had Jason sported some new ink but so had a few other of their friends that frequently stopped by. "If everyone else is getting tattoo's, count me in too," Cody said one night around Jason's kitchen table. Then when Jason bared his new ones, it was game on. It was now time to get some new ink so he could soon arrive at Jason's house to show off a new tattoo of his own.

They were both pretty high by the time talk of tattoos came around with Kevin. When Cody found himself with someone who loved opiates as much as himself, everything else became secondary. The high becoming much more important than the reason he came to the shop in the first place.

Kevin had quite the set-up. More advanced than anything he had seen previously but then again; it had been a few years since the skull tattoos in college. The manual labor of actually sketching the images onto laminate had been eliminated altogether. Kevin had a printer hooked up to the internet. "Wow", Cody thought, "The internet can get me drugs and tattoos faster. What a time to be alive!" He soon realized he would need that very technology's assistance; Kevin was so high he was nodding off! Kevin reached into a mini fridge located near his computer and grabbed an energy drink. There was nothing like the added feeling of opiates and caffeine. Shortly, being much more energized and alert they both picked out some skull images from Google and quickly got to work. When Cody pulled off his shirt the artist pointed out and started questioning his previous works of art. "What do those symbols mean?" Cody turned towards the nearest mirror and glanced at the Chinese symbols he'd had inked much earlier in life. They were done during a time when the thought of him even doing drugs would have struck him as ludicrous. Insane. That time was a distant fleeting memory as he turned back towards Kevin and chuckled. "Oh, these things? Faith and Courage. I got them a long time ago. Pretty lame huh" Cody replied. "Yeah, don't worry though we'll get them covered up with something cool in the next few sessions," said Kevin. "Awesome", Cody thought.

They went on to choose a skull wearing a gas mask to be placed in the middle of his torso. The beginnings of an apocalyptic scene Kevin had constructed in his drug educed stupor. The makings of a chaotic environment he soon found himself in. Below that, another skull image would be placed and that would conclude session number one. Kevin clicked print and the images began rolling out of the printer.

Cody drifted in and out of consciousness only from the feeling of something pressing on his torso. "How much have I snorted?" he thought. Enough to not really notice the multiple needles driving the ink into his stomach. Like that feeling when his girlfriend rubbed her nails down his chest and torso to wake him up. He wasn't waking up to a beautiful girl though. In a mid-elevated state, he found himself in a realm, not of the worldly kind. He found himself looking down upon himself. "Who was this person and where was he?" Cody stumbled in thought. The humming sound of the tattoo gun acting like the tick-tock of a hypnotist tool. It had in some way released him from his body to act as another opinion of himself. This bodily opinion was not so comatose and much more rational. "What are you doing and why are you here?" he heard himself ask. They were questions neither Cody nor his elevated state could answer. He found himself seeing images that simply painted a picture that became stained on the skin. It was dirty and filthy and nasty and everything disgusting and repulsive!

Just then the humming stopped, and he was transported back into himself. He blinked his eyes and realized it's him in the chair, the guy getting the repulsive tattoos in the picture. He wanted to run and never come back, find the nearest tattoo removal clinic, and burn the new ink from his skin. Instead, he got up from the tattoo chair and covered his new tattoos with bandages and ointment like the tattoos before. The standard procedure for helping heal the damaged skin. He then departed the House of Horror Shop.

The next day he returned with a pocket full of more pills and something new. His new drug of choice, Fentanyl. In a weird way, he was proud of it. Fentanyl wasn't something a lot of people who dabbled with opiates had ever done or even seen for that matter. It was considered a unicorn of the underground drug world, so he wanted to impress Kevin by showing off his rare product. He was putting tattoos on his body for no good reason other than to impress 'friends' that he wasn't sure he even cared about. Cody's lifestyle involved daily risk-taking behavior. He was constantly one-upped by a drugged-up acquaintance, a person just there to have fun with. He was always the one quick to show off in any way he could. If doing more drugs or drinking more alcohol was a contest, he'd always contended for first place. The tattoos were just another avenue to express his willingness to show off. "What is the real meaning to this tattoo obsession of mine?" he pondered as he walked into the shop. "Who am I really trying to gain attention from? Why?"

When Cody stepped into the house of horror shop for the second time, he stood in the mirror and inspected the work, slowly unraveling the bandages being careful not to pull off the healing skin. With drugs in hand, they both turned to head towards the glass topped coffin and skull-crushing device. Ironically and inconceivably the tattoo was beyond anything one's mind might humanly fathom. At least a drug free mind. It was 'dark and twisted' at its best. He threw the bandages and drugs atop the coffin to grab a $20 bill. As he began rolling it Kevin assisted by crushing the Oxy. Cody was saving the fentanyl surprise for later. A new form of payment he knew would continue sealing the deal for free ink, as nobody could resist it once they tried it and Cody knew the power it had. With the $20 bill rolled and the lines formed he placed the 20 into his good septum and plugged the other. As he bent down to snort a line off the top of the coffin he glanced to his left and caught a visual of the dried blood spattered on the white bandages. The image was a mockery straight from hell. The bandage, a vehicle of transport from Satan himself. "A message?" Cody's mind began to freak. The dried blood appeared to be a skull laughing at him. He grabbed the bandage and threw it in the trash. He knew then that "Tonight will be another long night."

If the Oxy they were starting with was considered a rainy day, then the fentanyl to come was a category five hurricane. Together Cody and Kevin would soon be entering the storm.

2

INNOCENT BEGINNINGS

Most of the seniors in high school are oblivious to the raw innocence they possess. I was clearly no exception. Only later in life do they in retrospect find that their problems weren't really problems at all. They were more like hurdles and less like roadblocks. Who am I kidding, for me they were speed bumps at best. Nothing could slow me down or hold me back. Those moments I lived in were the only thing that existed. My decisions became reflections of that impulsive time in my young life.

My first tattoo was to be a permanent mark, a symbol of my coming of age and independence. It would also be a reminder of the different directions my life could have gone at that moment in time. In the weeks following that tattoo, I would choose to be a collegiate athlete instead of going to boot camp in San Diego. A last-minute decision to play college football had overridden the decision to get on a bus and go to Camp Pendleton. I would soon be joining a team of men equipped with shoulder pads and a different type of helmet, one with a facemask. This decision, like the decision to get my first tattoo, was fueled by my friends who were constantly nagging me to give college a try. Like my mother, they didn't want to see me squander my opportunities away either. Not that they thought the military to be a bad option, they just knew the type of person I was.

I had been awarded many opportunities to visit campuses across the Midwest to play football but had instead gone behind my mother's back and enlisted in the Marine Corps, the infantry of course. I wanted to be on the front lines. Like the tattoo pricking my consciousness, the idea to enlist had been brought to fruition by a need to seek attention from my mother in any way I could, even if it meant joining the military behind her back.

Yet, I soon found myself arriving on the campus of Northwest Missouri State with an elated mother, excited that I was looking into giving college an opportunity at being a real option. After a successful visit, I called my Marine recruiter and asked what the repercussions of not getting on the bus would be. The bus that would be taking a group of young men to the airport bound of Camp Pendleton, San Diego. In short, he told me that despite my enlistment I would be in no real trouble if I decided not to show up for my leave date and get on the bus, so I didn't. I was soon going to depart for a different kind of camp, football camp.

Five years later I would receive a degree and every time I looked at the diploma it would join the tattoo in reminding me of the things that might have replaced it. The scary things associated with 'fighting for freedom' had I not chosen the exciting things in 'fighting for trophies'. Like the ink soaked into the paper of that college degree, I had a permanent reminder in the form of the ink lying in a layer of the dermis, just below the surface of my skin. Looking back, I can better see God's plan in it for me but at that moment in my life, I was just another 18-year-old kid doing my best to plant my feet, find my place, mark my ground, and fix any broken parts of my life by whatever means I felt worked.

I found myself riding out the last little bit of limelight that my senior year at Liberty High School could provide me. The epitome of 'Teenage Stardom'. I had it in my grasp. I was 'All-State Football' and Captain of the team. I had a ton of friends and many girls had befriended me. I was milking it for all it was worth, and then some. Yet, I didn't have it all.

The one thing I didn't have was a tattoo. I wanted one more than anything. The kids that did have them had risen to 'icon status' in high school. Seeming to be Rebels. Girls gawked when they would lift their sleeves to sport their new ink. Teachers and coaches just shook their heads in disbelief and disapproval. The tattoos made for the perfect tool on the ones sporting them. They would attract the girls and repel authority with a single mark. Two birds with one stone. I was very envious for more than one reason. My envy then turned to jealousy and my jealousy then turned to hatred for the wearer. In my mind's eye I thought, "I am the great athlete deserving the ultimate attention, not them", but without a tattoo, it wouldn't come. It seemed to take on a life of its own. It would go on to consume my thoughts. My fixation with getting a tattoo was obsessive. Lost in-class lectures I would even find myself doodling tattoo designs. The tattoo bug had sunk deep into my psyche. I found that it had slowly infected my circle of friends as well. We had all become obsessed with the idea of getting a tattoo. It reached a point where it seemed there was nothing that could save us from its pull. Then on a single day with a single decision, it was time. Time to get 'inked'.

Even with all my doodling artwork I still had no idea what I wanted. So, it would become one of those impulsive tattoos. The kind that happens from boredom and a little too much graduation money. I wanted a tattoo for the one main thing that it would provide me, attention. This made the content itself quite irrelevant and my struggle to decide even more fleeting. On the night of the decision to put 'needle to skin', I still had no real clue.

We found ourselves speeding through downtown Kansas City in search of the nearest tattoo shop. Though most people scout out certain artists that would exhibit qualities they like, that would not be us. The music in the car was cranked to the deafening audible of Incubus' "Wish you were here." The kind of music usually coupled with bad decisions and 'teenage spirit'. We were five close friends soon to be separated by college acceptance letters. We were out for our first taste of hormones combined with tattoo needles. Not yet realizing this had never in history proved to be a reliable combination for good decision making. Tonight, however, we embraced them. Scared, sure. Committed, absolutely. The soon-to-be works of art would become a time capsule of ink embedded into our skin. Memories to be drawn and trapped just below the surface. The shirts we wore, the songs we cranked, the car we cruised, the friends, these friends, my friends. All soon to be lost in our future lives apart, yet forever to be brought back within reach with a single glance at the soon-to-be tattoo on my left shoulder. The decision had been made knowing full well that it would piss my mother off, but I didn't care. I didn't need to care, now that I was in her good graces by making the decision to be a college football player instead of a Marine foot soldier.

Sometimes life gives us tattoo ideas, and then again sometimes tattoos are what give us ideas for life, at least for a moment in time. Those are the only two kinds. Either something inspires you to get a particular tattoo or the sheer excitement of getting one is inspiring. Tonight, we felt alive because of the adulterated acts we were about to commit on ourselves. When Jake yelled out through the music "Hey, Cody, that's it!" pointing up at the sign, we collectively knew it was perfect? It was a hole-in-the-wall tattoo shop called 'Freaks' on the upper floor of an old business building. Surrounded by numerous bars and sandwich shops, it was an awkward combination of businesses with their neon lights flashing in the windows. They seemed to be jockeying for a visual position in a competition by means of flash and flare. Clearly, they knew what attracted the novice crowd like us on these streets. What got our attention and what thrilled us. We were like moths sucked into the trance-like state by the bright lights of the sign, about to get zapped. We pulled up to the curb and piled out of the tiny Honda Civic. Bug-eyed and eager we stepped into the cold Midwestern air with a palpable combination of excitement and trepidation!

We were met with heavy clouds of sidewalk cigarette smoke as we charged into the building and began climbing the stairs. Two things caught my attention as we entered. The smell of antiseptic and the feeling of vulnerability in being 'rookies' surrounded by those much more 'experienced'. They were getting 'Inked', while we were getting 'Tattoos'! Our virgin skin revealed our state of no ink. I felt like we were the fresh dinner who just walked into the middle of a lion's den. "Stay calm, act normal, no sudden movements", I thought. As unsure as we were, we began doing what any clueless newbie entering a tattoo shop does. We began scouring the pictures plastered on the walls. We hoped to gain some inspiration as to what we wanted. As I meticulously studied the pictures, it wasn't long before I heard one of my friends, Brett, say he was getting a 'tribal' sun. I soon saw a similar sun I liked and thought "heck let's make it two". We seemed to be subconsciously moved by album covers that became conscious with suns. We loved music. I remembered then thinking "Why not let our first tattoos be a representation of the music?". Brett's would be inspired by Sublime, mine by Godsmack. So, within 20 minutes of stepping into 'Freaks', I had decided on an image that would be placed on me forever and headed for the front counter.

It seemed like that of a fast-food restaurant. Ordering not for a burger to eat, but for a piece of art to implant. I was nervous, to say the least with a few lingering trepidations trying to work at me. Should I show my mom or let her find out on her own?" I continued in thought.

We received and filled out the necessary questionnaires, presented our IDs, and signed away. We were told to wait as artists freed themselves up to sketch our tattoos onto laminate paper first. As we sat there, we made plans and fabricated stories about how cool we'd be all tattooed up in the final days of our senior year. Then a girl just ten feet in front of us squirmed and grimaced in pain. For the first time, I began regretting the decision to come. We had anticipated the pain but tried to override it by inviting stories of its coming mystery. I felt like I was witnessing a masochist sport and I was now about to join them on the field. People competing 'against' themselves. People who felt this type of therapy could enhance their life or cure whatever problem they had. Both were deemed worthy of such torture. Voluntary stab wounds from the needle of the tattoo gun. Regardless, to me it would appear that it would have to take on a hell of a life event to make such pain palpable. If I let my mind wander, I would see that the 'hell of a life event' I was experiencing was the recent divorce my mother and my stepdad Bill had gone through. I didn't care if the tattoo upset her. In my head I convinced myself she owed me this for the pain my siblings and I endured from the divorce. Thus, convincing myself that the tattoo was justified. It would allow me a little bit of push back from those situations I couldn't control. Fifteen years, almost my entire life, I was consumed by memories of a person that was one night gone. I had both hated him and loved him, but I had also been unaware of how to express either one appropriately in my youth. Bill had been a man that had shown me, in the youth of his own coming to marry my mom, how to win and how to push yourself to the absolute maximum. We had battled for the attention of my mother my entire life and I had always felt he had won, but now he was gone. "Was this a win by default?" I had been asking myself.

Just like that, Bill was gone. He had vanished in an instant. Overnight, I would attempt to be the new man of the house, but I never felt I held up to even the minimum standards. "Was I now a man?" I thought. The memories, both good and bad, were the only thing I had to try and remember of that past life with Bill. Now, just a best friend at best, I wasn't even sure what to call him. It didn't matter though; I hadn't seen him in a while. That life with my mom married to him, vanished. Now, the same vanishing was about to happen with my friends. The 'Tribal Sun' tattoo, although random and whimsical, it was now meaningful and intentional just the same.

"Why was I really here getting inked?" I continued to ponder. Then, one by one we were called up to the chair. Our tattoos were first placed on our bodies via laminate paper. The rough outlines were transferred onto our skin. The artist after having done hundreds before us, so we hoped, went through his standard checklist of items. Ink? Check. Clean needle? Check. Gloves? Check. By lying face down on a table, I had instilled more trust into that complete stranger with a needle than I had my physician. Both wielding needles, yet only one was truly certified in the study of anatomy. I really, deep-down was thinking "I can't believe I am here, but here I am nonetheless." My first step in joining this new sport. The sport of 'Getting Inked'.

I would then enjoy graduation and the precious few months with my friends showing off our new tattoos before summer football camp in August called me.

My Spiritual faith at that time was iffy at best. I was one of those 'Holiday Christians', covering the Christmas and Easter qualifiers. Not without putting up a decent fight to avoid even those. Like a cat being bathed, I would grab hold of any excuse not to go. My sun tattoo would soon become an incremental mark in my slowly distancing faith in God. For now, I was just an 18-year-old kid trying to fit further into life. There I was squeezing my hands to numb the pain of the needle driving ink below the surface of my skin. I did not know at the time that the little grip I still had with God was slipping. It would take a lot more than this to bring that reality above the surface. A lot more.

3

EMPOWER ME?

When the time neared to be dropped off for football camp the newness and excitement of the sun tattoo had already worn off. I now wanted something fresh, something people could see while I was on the football field wearing my pads. Some kids get their tattoos knowing that the repercussions from their parents will be less harsh if they are placed where they can be covered up by their clothes. Hidden for an extended amount of time only to be revealed to those who really appreciate ink. Others, bolder or foolish, have their tattoos so exposed that they have no sort of brake pedal for authoritative backlash. Then there are the ones that are not afraid to up the ante in a poker game of moral right and wrong. I was more like the latter. I was all in, as always. My inhibitions seemed to be weakening. The ones that sided with God anyway. I began to chase the 'high' of a rebellious nature despite those I felt I might be hurting. Mom and God. My dad hadn't seen them yet, but I was sure the next visit from him would reveal his loathing as well. Despite my internal awareness of the havoc I was about to inflict on myself and them, I did it anyway. My next tattoo decision was going to make my mother cry and I knew it. Yet, for some reason, I felt it was the price that had to be paid for me to rise, to survive, and thrive in the next level of my life. A life in constant need of attention and acceptance.

Mom already disliked the sun tattoo. This new tattoo was going to crush her. A moral regression in me was underway, fueled by my increasing attraction to fleshly vices. I didn't seem remotely interested in keeping it at bay or figuring out why or where it might lead me. All I cared about was hitting the college campus full of thousands of new eyes on my new tattoos.

This was my first real taste of addictive behavior in a long span of several addictive behaviors. The tattoos seemed the gateway to all the others. Sex, drugs, alcohol, and more.

During the experience of my first tattoo, I built a pretty decent rapport with the artist. I found that when you're sitting in a tattoo shop for extended amounts of time with someone, you naturally begin to converse with them. Especially when you've entrusted that person with a tattoo gun. It's strange at first. This complete stranger you have only just met, and they're now freely tasked with driving ink into your body. It has an indescribable intimacy that can only be rationalized if you've experienced it. The humming of the gun, the smell of the alcohol, and the pain of the needle all meld together in this kind of euphoric rush of emotions. A strange rush of endorphins, making all that seems wrong in the encounter come together and assist the darker side by making them feel, for the moment, right. Getting a tattoo was like that for me. Yet, time had not revealed that alcohol and drugs would involve the same intimacy.

I knew even as I got the first one that I'd want another. Maybe not real soon, yet soon enough to find it important to exchange numbers with my new friend, the artist. He told me to text him if I ever wanted another one, as if he too knew that I would. "No more waiting like tonight. Just figure out the day and time that works for you, text the picture over of what you'll want, and come on in." he said as if pre-coaching me before I left.

These tattoo express service lanes of which I had now entered get manufactured pretty quickly. I would learn that it's an artist's equivalency to a concierge service. In the cutthroat world of tattoos, there are never enough people in line and bills don't pay themselves. Walk-ins are a bonus but appointments via previous clients are an artist's bread and butter. Everyone who has numerous tattoos has a 'tattoo artist' on speed-dial. So, a couple of days before college move-in day, I sent some images of some Chinese symbols to 'my artist'. Sensing my urgency, he responded quite quickly, and we set up a time the following evening.

I arrived just the same, only alone this time. I climbed the familiar stairs that I had taken the month prior with my friends to enter this new world. I wasn't a newbie this time but the knot in my stomach seemed much more present. The provocative nature of getting the Chinese tattoos hadn't fully resonated with me yet, but for some reason, they tugged on me. In some way, I had chosen the symbols for Faith and Courage because at least those words when translated might soften the blow with my Christian mom. "At least they are not offensive," I thought. Then again, I didn't really care. It wasn't about the words themselves; it was about the look. No real worry I thought "Who in my life is ever going to ask about what they mean anyway, right?" I had now gotten to the point of wanting my tattoos to be seen, especially when I'd be on the football field in college. I remembered looking up to guys in the NFL from high school and seeing their tattoos thinking "Man, those look cool, I need some tattoos people can see". I felt uncommitted mentally but outwardly I refused to show it. I acted as if unphased and boldly greeted my artist. He once again began his standard checklist of the necessary procedures. The laminate paper was placed on my skin and the rough outlines transferred over. On the back of each arm at the triceps, he placed one large Chinese symbol. In my research for a new tattoo I had found that along with tribal symbols, Chinese tattoos were at their peak of popularity in America. Koi fish and Cherry Blossom flowers were also popular, but Chinese symbols were really the things to have, and have I would.

Everything in this country seems to have its phases, including tattoos. The only difference between a tattoo phase and say a clothing phase; you can't donate the tattoo to your local Goodwill and then hit the mall for an upgrade. It's with you for life.

Inking the sun on my back had hurt little, however it was not the same for the needles penetrating the soft tissue on the back of my arms. I recalled the girl I had seen in the chair earlier that summer when I had gotten the sun tattoo with my friends. I could now relate to what I had seen in her. I was the one now squirming and grimacing as 'my artist' worked away. As he finished one arm and went to the next, I knew there was no turning back. The damage was done, but "man are they going to look cool at college!" I thought as I endured the pain. I just gritted my teeth and did what I had done so well up to that point in my life…persevere.

When the tattoos were finished and I put my shirt on, they set on my arms just low enough to be seen with, but not fully. In my football pads, they would clearly be completely seen. "Perfect!" I thought. These would be a conspicuous segue into the constant sought-after question they ask when they see just one, "Do you have any more tattoos?" I sensed and hoped this would prove especially useful with the women I would encounter, becoming my new icebreaker to the conversation. "It would surely end with me removing my shirt to show off the sun tattoo, right?" working to convince myself.

Then the inevitable happened, Mom saw the new tattoos. She just looked at them then looked at me and shook her head, saying nothing. She didn't even ask what they meant. It was probably the worst thing she could have done. That thing parents do when the disappointment in their child has no words, and no words are needed to express what they don't want to say. It cuts deeper than any spanking when you're a toddler or any grounding when you're in your teens. It's the eye contact and the head shake that screams "I raised you better than that and now you're on your own". Mom performed her silence masterfully as she walked away. It hurt. It hurt far worse than the pain I'd experienced in getting them inked. The sting from her, just as permanent a few days later as the scabbed over tattoos on the back of my arms were.

Then came the awkward silence the day she dropped me off at college. We unpacked my clothes and other things into my dorm room, making several trips back and forth, not saying much to each other as we passed in the halls. Eventually, she cried. After we hugged, she got back in her car and drove back to Kansas City. I sensed that like most parents do when they drop their kids off at college, she was sad that her kid was gone. But she was also fearfully happy for the next chapter that was to unfold in my life. Yet, she also had some added stress; she knew deep down, from what she was seeing in me that I was on a dangerous journey. I felt she saw the tattoos as a visible representation of a dark road I was headed down. Then again, I was off at college "What could she do?" I soon settled in with that thought.

After waving goodbye to her from my dorm window I move to the mirror on the back of one of the doors and stared at my new tattoos. I twisted and turned and flexed my triceps to get the best view of them, "Faith and Courage" in Chinese. As I looked, I thought of my faith for the first time in a long time. Of my relationship and trust in God and His Mercy. I felt as though I was seeing none of that in my life. My Mom was moving to Philadelphia for a new job opportunity and my Dad was still up in Iowa. I was feeling I had nobody I could turn to as I stood in my new dorm in my new college town. I felt more alone than ever. Yet, I knew I would make friends and gain acceptance soon enough. I was sure of that. With my high school friends and coaches now gone, it would take a little bit of that Courage. A whole lot of what I'd already absorbed from High School would help me find new people who would accept me. I had learned the power and quality of attraction, charisma, and I would soon put it to good use.

4

THE CREEP OF DARKNESS

College for me was a time of self-discovery, as it is for most young adults. It was that precious time in life when I began to look back at myself for the first time and try to understand why I was the way I was? What shaped me, molded me into the person that was staring back in the mirror? It was then that I began to make self-proclaiming statements of myself, shaped through the views of other's opinions.

"What does the world think of me? Am I acceptable enough?"

We don't realize that left unchecked we lose sight of the view that matters most, Gods and replace it with our friends. What a tradeoff. The longer these skewed views are allowed to continue, the farther we remain from the true vision of our absolute best. That vision is God's vision of us. It's a vision of ourselves, that's filled with love and joy, not outer beauty masked with physical tangibles. I was becoming, if not already blind to this. As a football player in college, I began lifting and building muscle with my teammates. I gained a lot of eye contact and comments from guys and girls in regard to the size I was putting on. I latched on to those looks and statements finding great validation of myself in them. I was getting high from the attention of people who could care less about who I was as a person but cared more about the size of my chest. Comment after comment allowed me to push myself deeper and deeper into a world of bodily aesthetics, bodybuilding. I kept it to myself that my inner strength was non-existent all the while building my outer shell of strength for all to see. I didn't have time to look at that as compensating for my inner weakness, for to even let such a thought into my conscious psyche would be like surrendering. Something that had now become foreign to me. Something that in its avoidance motivated me. Something that I would not allow to come from my lips. "Cody Lanus does not surrender! He prevails!"

Then, as if on cue the darkness that harbors demons began to spread like a wildfire inside me. It would only be a matter of time before they latched on to me and made a home inside, or rather on my chest. The people I began to surround myself with were of course, no different. I heard once that "you're a median of the people you surround yourself with." I was surrounding myself with college football stars. Especially the ones who got drunk, used drugs, and had sex with lots of women. They became my new best friends and to my delight had lots of tattoos.

The fact is that college football players are treated pretty well, especially in the nightlife scene. Not world celebrity status but for a small Midwestern college town, it was close enough to feel the same. My friends and I frequented one specific bar, especially after game days. The drinks were cheap, the music was loud, and the girls wore next to nothing. Our testosterone was left to roam mentally free, a temptation we couldn't resist. We became its best representatives. We were constantly under supervision and worried about being kicked off the team, so we did a good job of keeping each other in check. The fight's happened, but rarely when we were there. When they did, it was usually one of us superstars breaking it up. We were good for business, eventually building a decent Rapport with the owner. He liked having us around for obvious reasons as we helped his business in more ways than one. The women came for the prospects of the eye candy and the ruffians stayed away for fear of the wrath of the eye candy's muscle. After hours when the bar was cleared, we'd have a couple of drinks with the manager Ben. He routinely joked about us working security. We laughed off the idea our entire freshman year. Kicking drunk kids out of a bar seemed like the last thing we wanted to do. We still had a lot of bars to get kicked out of ourselves. This early role reversal seemed strange at best. Then during my sophomore year, my football scholarship's 'living funds' started to run out and accepting Bar Security as a job was becoming a very real possibility. "Why not start putting this size of mine to good use?" I questioned. So it was.

The job would lead to more than just some extra spending money, it would lead to my chest covered in tattoos. By now the world had moved into the 'skull phase' of tattoo artistry and that's the world I would join. Following this trend in popularity became my niche. It turned out to my surprise that there was a tattoo shop across the street from the bar. I just never realized it until I became part of the Security Team because my previous intoxication level never allowed for it. I was that oblivious. I never went to the bar sober, and I definitely never left that way either. Working there opened my eyes to notice my surroundings. The tattoo shop door was no more than fifty feet from the bar's door, yet I had never seen it. Now, I stood between both doors while doing my job. Literally immersed, I was dead in water of restraint. Every day I would take I.D.s at the door and every day that flashing sign would call my name. Tattoos. Tattoos. Tattoos.

With my rent paid and groceries bought I walked out of the bar most nights with a pocket full of cash and nothing to do. I remember sitting in my car contemplating which girl I'd text, what after party I would attend, or if I wanted to go home; lay in my apartment and wait for the strobe lights and bass from the bar to subside from my consciousness. Most nights it took some work, usually via Nyquil or some other over-the-counter tranquilizer. Anything to slow my racing mind down. I lived life in hyper speed and downers would become my drug of choice. I had begun to use sleeping pills regularly. There was something insistent about them that was immerging in my head, but I didn't understand it. As if a voice, so to speak. Whatever it was the pills could quiet it down as well as help me get to sleep.

Because of this, my drug-induced sleep pattern seemed to never allow me to reach the deeper stages of REM, leaving me still exhausted by morning. But between the daily tackling drills and my second home as a night club, that's usually what it took for me to get any. It's like my brain was being squeezed in a vice and never reaching equilibrium. I could only wonder how I was managing to sit through lectures, let alone how I was going to obtain a degree.

I lost track of the concussions after the third. I usually drank three red bulls on any given night. As I sat in my car one evening listening to my caffeine-induced heart beat out of my chest, I decided I had watched the flashing Tattoo sign long enough. It was time.

When I entered, the first thing I noticed was that the scene of people and chairs full of squirming victims I remembered from my first shop did not exist. This new shop was full of people drinking and a haze of smoke that I knew from the aroma wasn't of the tobacco kind. A red flag I was now familiar with, but ignored, nonetheless. "Where are the pictures plastered on the walls? The smell of anti-septic and alcohol familiar with every shop I'd been in?" I thought. As I was about to introduce myself to the gentleman that was walking straight at me, he spoke first, letting me know that he was the owner. We grabbed a couple of chairs and he proceeded to pull out a picture album of previous tattoos he had done. A collection of his best work to show potential clients his talents and capabilities. As I flipped through the pictures, I tried to act impressed, but they were horrific. Nothing resembled anything that could remotely be considered good art. The lines were messy, the art elementary, even the letters were sloppy and uneven. I should have put the album down and walked out. I should have turned around immediately and went home to my comatose cocktail. This was another red flag. How many more did I need? Clearly, two wasn't enough as I found myself doing the most illogical thing possible. Once again, I was going to put blind faith in a stranger with a tattoo gun. Even into one who was more of a novice than the first artist at 'Freaks'. How does the saying go, I thought to myself, "Jesus takes the wheel." At that moment I was hoping it was Him and not another.

As I flipped through the album I stopped abruptly when I got to a skull design that caught my eye. I proceeded to discuss with him a scene I was thinking about lately and now interested in, one of good and evil. It would be skulls on one side and angels on the other. I sensed, though I did not say it out loud, that it would be something to represent the life I lived to be placed on each side of my chest. Wings protruding from them up towards my shoulders. A variation of what I'd surprisingly learn later is called a "Dead Head." An image made famous by the Motorcycle Club known as the Hells Angels. "Whoops!" By the time I would learn of that revelation, it would be already inked on my chest.

I was quite unaware or was just ignoring the fact that some darkness had slowly begun to take over my life. It came with one poor decision after the next, and nothing seemingly in my grasp was to slow it down. Like a pure white flake of snow that begins a tumble and picks up momentum until it's an avalanche consuming trees and rock. Like the fool who finds one foot in the fire. He feels it burning but for some reason, he doesn't remove it. Instead, he does the exact opposite of what a rational mind should do. He gives up and jumps in with both feet.

I'm not sure which red flag I was on when he took out the sharpie and began drawing on my chest. Without the customary laminate paper placed perfectly on my skin; he had somehow convinced me he was better at free handing it. If the photos were any proof of that I couldn't tell. Either way, I went with it. I laid down on the chair as several spectators with at least a contact high gathered around to watch the show. I was going to be the entertainment for the evening. A willing participant to what they all probably knew was a poor decision. With no ambition to enter a battle that wasn't their own, they looked on like a medieval crowd about to witness a beheading. When he began prepping the gun, I was at least cognizant enough to double-check and make sure he put in a fresh needle. "What number of 'red flag' was I on?" I sensed trying to ask myself. Something was repeatedly telling me to run away, yet I continued to ignore it as if paralyzed. I was far from being in a position to recognize that voice was God's warning. Eve loved apples, and I loved tattoos. Both were disguised as tantalizing treats. Both found on Earth, the apple, and the tattoo, testing the will to resist. Not a chance that would happen this night. As he fired up the tattoo gun, I laid back and looked up at the faces around me surrounded by a cloud of smoke. I closed my eyes and geared up for a five-hour tattoo session with what I soon would realize was a 'heavy-handed' artist, the industry's phrase for someone who pushes down on the gun too hard when they tattoo, making the process that much more painful. At the moment of recognition that there was no turning back all I could think to say to one of the spectators was, "Let me get a hit of that!".

That night was the first night I would mark in my memory that I surrendered to the wrong voice and the battle I experienced that led up to it. Remembering the decision I made despite the unaccepted sound of the Voice of Reason that had been reverberating through my head.

I had ignored that voice of reason previously in my life but on this night, it was much more obvious to me. As if someone was wanting me to record this process. I was beginning to recognize that in an instant the adversary's voice could take over my thoughts. It was making a home deep inside me and setting up shop within it. It was now convincing me that my illegitimacy was justified. It was now convincing me that these skull tattoos were ok. It had now been a couple of years since my Mom had dropped me off and I no longer cared about what she thought. A new woman's voice in my head now controlled me and was instilling in me the ability to live with a lack of control in myself. These new skull tattoos were the very representation of that new voice. It was becoming evident by looking in the mirror and seeing the demonic artwork scribbled on my chest. I remember looking in the mirror and smiling as if I was party to it, and accepting it was okay. Yet, at the same time inside, somewhere deep within me, I knew it was insidious. Those close to me would ask me "What were you thinking?" and all I could say was "There's more to come!" as if professing something worse in the future would make this current seem better, more acceptable. I wanted to be covered and I wanted it as soon as possible. "Who was I becoming?" I thought often but pushed it away as fast as it came. I was infatuated with not just one tattoo but ink from neck to toes. I wanted to keep the skull theme throughout too. "Who was I trying to impress?" I pondered many times. It wasn't my family or friends, teammates, or girls. At this point even they began to question my sanity. It was something much more powerful, an entity that was pulling itself closer. One I couldn't seem to shake.

With my shirt off standing in the shop looking in the three-way mirror I caught myself in a trance-like state staring at the skulls on my chest. Finally snapping out of it, I turned to look at my triceps in the mirrors like I had in my dorm room a couple of years earlier. As I saw those symbols I was reminded of many things, that first day in this town being one of them. Despite my new mistake, at least God was there in the form of the Chinese symbols attempting to speak to me, Faith and Courage. The very tattoos that marked a time when I had many more morals than the ones now being displayed. "Was there still Hope?" I briefly pondered. There was no time for an answer as I began laughing when a girl on a mission, covered in tattoos grabbed my arm and began pulling me out the front doors. I didn't even know her name. There was only time for one more glance, Faith and Courage.

5

THE FIRST TASTE OF ADDICTION'S LINK

Cody sat quietly on the couch. He was depressed from the unbelievable idea spinning through his head. The idea of having to miss the rest of his High School's sophomore 'football' season. He could only hope to not miss any of the upcoming 'basketball' seasons on top of it. He sure didn't want to let the man down who had instilled such a work ethic in him, Coach Stirtz. Cody really looked up to him in other ways too, especially the mental release he provided ever since the fighting at home between his mom and stepdad had escalated.

The coach was the first 'Christian' he looked up to. Never swearing or yelling, he was able to gain respect through his actions. Around Coach Stirtz, Cody not only played hard, but he carried himself with dignity and respect as well. Just like his coach did. Now coaches and fellow players were telling him to 'Get better." So, 'getting better' is what Cody now intended to do. Until this.

He sat there just staring at the bottle in front of him on the coffee table. His elbow was really killing him, throbbing intensely. The doctor said it was a complete dislocation. He'd been carried off the field to an ambulance, screaming like a little baby the entire way. Cody remembered feeling the awkwardness in his arm as a helmet made its abrupt contact with his elbow and was surprised that the pain hadn't set in immediately. He remembered wondering for a few brief moments to himself "Why are the players running off the field, yelling for the athletic trainer in what sounds like horror-filled bursts?" Then his name was suddenly attached to the pleas, "Cody needs help! It looks really bad!" He wasn't really sure what they were yelling about until he decided to join the others and look down to see his elbow sticking out, quite out of natural order.

There was a ten-minute period between the ambulance loading him up and the first needle that entered his vein. A needle he heard the paramedics in the ambulance say was filled with Morphine. Despite the chaos, he had remembered wondering if he had heard the word before. His shocked brain couldn't answer it. "Ok, Cody we're going to give you some 'Morphine' to help numb the pain" the paramedic had said. The moment the drug hit him Cody knew for sure it was something he had never felt before, yet it was so powerful that he remembered sensing a wish that he had. At the hospital, a quick x-ray would soon prove it to be a complete dislocation. Then came the pleasant procedure of the doctor quickly manipulating it back into its more natural place. Even through the morphine it felt more like 'yanking' and not 'manipulating', though he was no longer whining like a little baby!

Now sitting on the couch in a cast with a swollen arm, he continued staring at the bottle. From what the doctor said, and the label confirmed it was a drug called Percocet. It seemed to be staring back at him from less than ten feet away. He hated pills and had avoided them at all costs. This stemmed from the fact that his mom didn't really believe in medicating things. She was more of the "rub some dirt on it!" kind of mom therefore not much medicine was used in Cody's household. It would seem that growing up as a small-town Iowa girl with several brothers and sisters would be the beginning of what toughened his mom. A toughness that clearly carried on and now showed in her own children.

He continued contemplating these foundational stands on drugs she took as he stared at the bottle of pills which were still staring back at him. His mother had actually stowed them away while she and Cody's sisters went out shopping. Then, all alone as he began remembering the feeling of the morphine, Cody wondered if the pills might provide the same 'euphoric' feeling while it relieved his elbow pain. So, in an attempt to find out he had retrieved them out of the cabinet, under the disguise that he was only going to read the label. "The doctor had called them 'painkillers' but what really are they?" he thought. Cody read the fitness magazines for some time now and followed the guys he believed to be pinnacles of fitness. "They wouldn't take pills if they were in my situation, would they?" Cody thought. "But, if the pills were anything like the power of the morphine, they sure would be helpful," ratcheting up the convincing self-talk. "Besides, I won't need them all, just a few to manage the pain while my elbow heals," not seeming to be able to stop his self-musing.

Cody's mom soon came through the front door with his sisters, and they immediately scattered to their rooms to tear into their new clothes. Then she popped into the living room to check on her injured son. As she neared the couch, she saw her son in a condition that she wasn't quite sure she'd seen him in before. As new as this was for her to see him like this, Cody instantly had a similar reaction to her face. It showed, without saying a word that she realized what he had done. That knowledge seemed to awake in her past feelings she had long kept buried and seeing these unfamiliar expressions on her son's face triggered them. It was confirmed when Cody looked up at her and foolishly, through a tooth-clenched grin said "Hey, mom, what's up?".

As Maichelle came closer, she hesitantly replied "Hey Hun, are you ok?" Then as if hit with the reality of it she took a quick step backward. Cody saw her do it as if it was an instinctual retreat. Hoping to mask what he now knew she saw he casually responded, "Oh yeah, I feel great. How was shopping, what'd you buy?"

That line of conversation became secondary to the elephant in the room. He knew it was there, but he continued his deflection anyway not realizing he was about to make the elephant bigger. "Hey mom, I was thinking. How pissed would you be if I ever got a tattoo?" not stopping to breathe "One of my buddies at school got one and everyone loves it." His mom let the remaining shopping bags she held in her hand drop to the floor. She knew her son had indeed taken something. Through everything they had endured together, Maichelle had raised him better than that and a fifteen-year-old should be trusted at home with medicine in the cabinet. "How many did you take?" is all he heard. "Two, just two" Cody grinned back. "Give me the bottle, I'm hiding them. If you absolutely need them then ask me, otherwise, just take a couple of Tylenol. You're tough, you don't need this junk," she snapped as she jacked the bottle from him. No discussion, no coaching, and no compassion. Just the familiar 'tough love' commands of his mom.

He didn't know if it was his will or the drugs, but he ignored her passionate profession and continued smiling. No "Yes ma'am" followed. He remained fixated on his previous question. "Hey mom, you didn't answer my question. What would you do if I ever got a tattoo?" Just then she answered her ringing phone, turned back towards the door grabbing the bags with her free hand, and became lost in an instant argument with the man Cody knew was on the other end of the call. His stepdad Bill. The man who had forced Cody to call him dad his entire life. He flashed back to the time when he was with his real biological father and accidentally referred to Bill as "Dad" right in front of him. It stung his father Larry really bad, and Cody had always felt responsible, hoping to never repeat it again. Coming back to the reality of the moment and listening to her on the phone, he knew these heated arguments she was having with Bill were had been escalating as of late and were becoming much more frequent. But, for the first time, in his new drug-induced state, Cody felt as if the arguing didn't really matter. It just seemed 'ok' to him, even in the wrongness of it.

A perfect storm was brewing, and he didn't know it. One involving his physical and emotional pain that was now linking in search of resolve. The need to subdue it. The pain of it that was normally in Cody's stomach from such arguments wasn't there. He didn't feel the previous need to engage in the argument that his mom was having on the phone. He stood and as she moved, he asked her calmly over her conversation, "Hey mom, is everything ok?"

Maichelle pulled the phone from her now reddened face and looked in Cody's direction and chose to ignore his compassionate question. Instead, she finally answered the tattoo question.

"Don't even think about it.".

6

THE EXECUTIONER'S PORTAL

...INWARD

After chopping and snorting a couple of Oxy each they made their way to Kevin's computer. Cody passed the trash and glanced down, fearful that the blood-stained skull would be staring back up at him. He felt relieved as the nervousness in his stomach disappeared when he saw the bandages were crumpled up, revealing no laughing skull like before. With no scary representation or demonic insinuation present, he turned from the trash can with a smile on his face. With the drug's now working their magic, he felt as if the center of the universe revolved around him. He felt amazing. He felt unstoppable. His universe was now alive, right in the tattoo shop. Alive, right in the center of Omaha Nebraska.

In his Oxy-induced state, for the second night in a row, he and Kevin began searching the internet for images suitable to continue the chosen skull theme. Google had no shortage of possibilities in that arena, so they dug right in. Cody was sporting a tank top upon arrival but now leaned over the computer desk shirtless making it easier to look at the screen possibilities and the ink of Kevin's handiwork. While scouring the images rapidly filling the screen Kevin took a quick glance toward Cody and began chuckling. "What's so damn funny?" Cody thought but didn't speak. Then he realized that the Faith and Courage symbols on his arms were the source of Kevin's laughter. The drugs were clearly working as evident by Kevin's shoulders bouncing up and down with every exaggerated laugh and trying to talk between gulps for air. "We've really got to get those Chinese symbols covered man," he composed himself enough to speak. Cody had slowly but surely begun to buy into the negative comments that they were, indeed, pretty lame. "Maybe next week we can do a couple more back-to-back sessions and clean that up." Kevin continued. With that, the symbols went from lame to a full-blown joke in Cody's mind. Now feeling some internal need to impress Kevin and further gain his acceptance he spoke up, "Yeah man, let's do some arm sleeves. Some 'skull collages' down both arms, that'll get um covered". Re-engrossed in the skull images on the screen Kevin merely nodded while speaking in agreement, "Yeah man, arm sleeves sound like a sick idea bro."

Cody was less than certain his bosses at Boys Town would approve of all this. He knew full well that they had a "No Visible Tattoos' policy but didn't know if it mentioned 'Questionable Themes' like skulls. But it was more than his current 'elevated' state that kept him from really caring at that moment. He had already lived outside the company's policy by sleeping with a subordinate and was certain that in the fine print it said he wasn't supposed to be dealing drugs. Though he always wondered what would happen if his superiors found out about any of his current debaucheries. It didn't seem to make much sense worrying about adding the new 'skull theme' to the wonderment. Yet deep inside he knew if any part of his double life came to light, keeping a job at Boys Town would be the least of his concerns.

His mom would be disappointed too, but he seemed to be ok in not giving a shit about that either. The rationale was that she lived halfway across the country in Philadelphia with her new family. It might as well have been a million miles from Omaha. She had started a new family after Cody had left high school and that was keeping her well occupied. She had quickly remarried after the divorce from Bill and Cody hadn't seen her for a few years. The way his life was going he probably wouldn't see her for a few more either. She'd most likely catch wind of the tattoos on Facebook. Then, by the time their monthly phone call came around he figured she'd probably have already processed the anger. "Better yet, this may give her a reason to actually call sooner." Cody thought. "Either way she'll get over it." he continued. He now was lost in thought of his mother as he numbly was watching Kevin scroll away lackadaisically on the computer.

Soon Cody's Dad Larry popped into his thoughts. He would hate them too. In a small town, a hard-working blue-collar man, his dad, was raised by Catholics. One wasn't supposed to get tattoos anywhere on their body and his dad would never dream of it for himself let alone his son. Cody knew he wasn't his dad though and most definitely hadn't been raised with the same rules. Most of the rules in Cody's life had been established not by the Church or a Priest but by coaches through athletics. Now that he had been out of sports for a few years, even those rules now seemed easier to bend or break.

Cody had never been the best candidate at building tight relationships other than on the gridiron. His parents didn't' seem to be either. Not with themselves and surely not much with him. Some semblances of a relationship certainly existed in each of their lives but nothing truly meaningful had ever been built. At least not grounded in any real substance that he could come up with at that moment. He loved his parents more than anything, but he always felt like some piece of the puzzle was missing. One he couldn't quite pinpoint. Cody felt in a way that his dad did the best he could. Yet, with his dad's always demanding job and their personal bonds only built around seeing each other during Holidays, it was hard to really see the potential his Dad could have on his life.

"Why should I worry about what they think?" Cody concluded as he continued staring at the skull images on the screen. Though far away in thought he had been pointing from time to time to acknowledge Kevin's interest in certain pictures. "They haven't even been here to my home in Omaha yet." the thought of them now irking Cody. After he and Lauren had split a few years back, at 27 years old Cody had purchased a nice home and he pridefully wanted to show it off to them more than he had ever imagined. Sure, he knew it was the same house the drugs were being sold from, but they didn't need to know that. Besides, if they ever did come, he would have Brandi clean it up in a jiffy for him. Truth be told, now thinking on it, Cody cared more about Brandi's opinions in regard to the skull sleeves than his own parents. She was the sweetheart girl that had been living at Cody's house the past few months. Allowing himself a cavalier thought "The sex and house cleaning was a decent enough tradeoff for the rent and groceries I am providing. With the bonus of performing one of the most tedious of tasks, labeling steroid vials."

Contemplating these things while lost in the glow of the computer screen he was jolted back to reality when Kevin barked "There it is, that's the one!" Kevin had stopped at the 'Five Finger Death Punch' album cover and had it enlarged on the screen. If anything would fit the theme Cody was trying to go for, this was it? The image of the world seemingly in ashes, smoldering hot with apocalyptic men in gas masks meandering about. "That's what you need dude, that's what your missing" Kevin continued in excitement, "Brass Knuckles". The knuckles were strewn across the top of the album cover. With the Oxy now climaxing through his blood, Cody did what he had done a few moments before, he agreed by saying "Sure man, those look sweet." As if now given free liberty at creativity Kevin said "Let's do the brass knuckles above the skull gas mask. I'll leave some empty area on the knuckles for the smoke from the gas masks to come up through when we come back and finish it. The smoke will be the last thing that will piece this all together." It was now visualized and decided. Time to begin phase two.

The previous night's work had been halted due to sleep deprivation. The skull wearing the gas mask still remained unfinished on Cody's stomach. Within 24 hours he had escalated from wanting a tattoo to impress his friends to now having a couple more on his body and the workings of several more being concocted in their minds for the following week. "Is all this being driven by the Oxy or is this really me?" once again Cody found himself asking internally. "Have I gotten myself in over my head?" Before any answer came his mind switched to an interesting thought. "Kevin seems to be doing an excellent job of keeping me as a 'soon to return' client with just a couple bumps of Oxy. Maybe he doesn't need the Fentanyl after all?"

...OUTWARD

For the second night in a row, the printer began spewing out their desired image from Google. An image of world desolation that would soon be transferred to Cody's skin. Unlike Cody's previous tattoos it wasn't a skull. It would be brass knuckles, inspired by the 'Hard Rock' album cover, to be placed on his sternum above yesterday's 'gas mask-wearing skull'. They decided to leave the finger areas open in the brass knuckles where smoke would rise, lazily drifting through the knuckles, to be inked in a future session. Although it had been chosen quite randomly, Cody thought it was decently creative. Even through the slower thought process that came with their snorting too much Oxy.

As the printer released the paper Kevin grabbed it and stood up. His knees appeared weak from his impairment, so he slowly staggered towards his workstation. Cody followed suit, shuffling behind him. Knowing his position, he plopped himself down next to Kevin's workstation on the tattoo chair. He felt the cold artificial feeling of the plastic from the chair mix with the warmness of this body, melding together a feeling he wasn't quite sure how to process. Cody forced himself into a hypnotic state as Kevin began opening and closing drawers gathering items in preparation for the main event and another long night.

Kevin fidgeted with this and that, swearing under his breath as Cody continued staring forward in his trance-like state. Becoming lost once again in past memories he recalled the times when he actually became nervous before getting tattooed. Now, with a combination of experience, drugs, and the 'lack of care' in his corner, those nerves no longer existed. Snip. Snip. Cody heard faintly as Kevin cut the brass knuckles out of the paper. He had a euphoric feeling that was now beginning to engulf him. That warm blanket of comfort seemed to remove any doubt, allowing him to say, "fuck it!" despite the dual forms of self-corruption taking place: Tattoos and drugs. "These are but tattoos and a little Oxy. The minimal aspects of my now estranged life" he thought. Unblinking, he continued in a fixated glare, unaware of the horror movie posters in front of him. They had gone from being horrible to being normal. He wondered once again about Boys Town. This time what the kids would think of his skull tattoos. "I'm sure they'll be intrigued, as most kids are, but what kind of example will I be setting? What kind of role model will I be?" He realized he was sitting forward-pondering all of that when Kevin pulled him back, forcing him to lay down. "Hey dude, snap out of it," Kevin said. He pressed the paper with the brass knuckles on his sternum, doing his best to center it. When the placement was correct Kevin slowly pulled the paper off. The rough outline of brass knuckles was now all that remained. "Perfect" Kevin whispered. Cody shook himself from his opiate-induced cloud for his final commitment and relaxed.

Pushing through the noise of the buzzing of the gun and the recent thoughts of his impulsive decisions, he closed his eyes. There was to be no "Are you ready?" type of conversation. Kevin simply began. When the gun fired up, they both knew what time it was. The needle, going in and out of Cody's skin as in previous sessions began to soothe him. The blood Kevin repeatedly wiped off Cody's sternum, was living proof that the needle actually was indeed puncturing him. Needles of more than one kind had now become a pretty constant thing in Cody's life. As he lay there enduring the sting of this one, he thought of the other kind. The ones he'd used in his home. The used ones he kept in a grocery bag in the small cabinet above the stove, thrown up there after every injection of this and that kind of drug. He was now up to a few needles a day between the steroids and other drugs he regularly injected. Cody was no stranger to the sharp thin metal devices. He laid there remembering his injection of steroids just before coming to see Kevin. Recalling the fact that the grocery bag was full he attempted to make a mental note to text Brandi to have her dispose of them. He felt they did a decent enough job making sure nobody got poked handling the garbage by usually pushing them into an empty milk jug and taping the top shut. It wasn't hospital-grade safety, but it was better than just throwing them in the trash. Cody continued enduring the tattoo needles from Kevin's gun, thankful they were much smaller than the 1.5 inch, 23-gauge needles Cody personally used. "Text Brandi" he kept repeating to himself.

Kevin finished the brass knuckles in about 90 minutes. This was quite fast Cody thought but soon remembered the motivator that made it possible. They had taken a 're-up' break and snorted more Oxy in the middle of the operation. Some significant enough pain had set in by that time, justifying those extra lines of Oxy, at least for Cody. Kevin's justification was of a different kind.

Now with the job completed they got up from their respective chairs and staggered back over to Kevin's coffin desk. Kevin popped the mini-fridge open and grabbed a couple of Red Bulls. Tossing one in Cody's direction it hit him in the chest and fell to the floor. He was so high his response time wasn't even close. Laying there on the floor they both looked at the can and in unison began laughing. "Nice Catch" Kevin yelled. "Shut up man, you know I'm a bit fucked up,"

Cody barked back defensively. He never claimed to be a receiver in his football days either. Tonight was proving no different. Cody grabbed the can from the floor and set it on the coffin, waiting for the fizz to settle before opening it. This would prove to allow the time needed for an idea to pop into his head. "I've got something else you might like, man!" he said to Kevin, the idea now finding a voice. Staring into the mirror on the wall Cody was admiring his new tattoos. He rubbed the necessary copious amounts of ointment on the new one and lightly touched up the day-old ones as he waited to see if Kevin would take the bait. He wouldn't be disappointed. "What are you talking about?" Kevin replied. After taking a hit of Red Bull Cody pulled a baggie from his shorts pocket. With the new tattoos no longer having any immediate interest, Cody turned away from the mirror and faced Kevin head-on. The bag was now at shoulder length and he waved it back and forth in front of Kevin like a treat for a pet. "Don't worry about what it is, just trust me," Cody replied. Intrigued Kevin slammed the Red Bull down next to Cody's on the coffin, small droplets erupting from the silver and blue can. He snatched the bag from Cody's hands and began greedily pouring out Oxy-sized lines to snort. Knowing the minuscule amounts it actually took to get high from this 'surprise drug' Cody quickly intercepted Kevin, grabbing him by the shoulders like a toddler. "Easy Bro, this is Fentanyl, not to be fucked with!". Taking a key from his pocket, he scooped up a tiny amount on the end of it, about an eighth of the size of one Oxy line. "This is it; this is all it takes," Cody said. Speechless, wide-eyed, and mesmerized by what he had just heard Kevin was only able to murmur a couple of words indicating his comprehension of the power of what he was about to be a part of. "I'm down".

...DOWNWARD

Taking charge, Cody held the tiny key bump for Kevin to go first. He had a pretty good idea of how much to do as he and Jason had been at it for a few months now. Cody also knew that his tolerance was much greater than Kevin's. It would take very little to unleash her power on this his first-time user. In fact, it was such a tiny amount that you could barely see the powder accumulated at the end of the 'Chrysler 300' key. The same key to the car that screamed drug dealer. Cody regretted buying it due to the numerous times he'd been pulled over in it. He hoped tonight wouldn't be one of those times as he continued holding the key towards the eager recipient. Kevin, confident in his drug-taking abilities stepped up to the plate. His faith in Cody's drug dosing abilities seemingly just as confident. The smile on his face portrayed this as he proceeded to plug the desired nostril. "Not like he'd even need any real power to sniff that tiny amount." Cody thought. With a quick sniff, the Fentanyl was gone. Only a brief moment remained for Kevin.

The excitement in Cody's body as he now held a tiny key bump for himself was much more euphoric than anything still left in his system from the Oxy. The thought of what was to come from the Fentanyl had that kind of power. Cody was feeling its full force as he stood there in front of Kevin, feeling the high of the drug before he even did it. The cells in Cody's body, absolutely aware of what was about to happen. A bead of sweat now formed on his brow. He knew in that brief moment Kevin was now feeling something that he'd probably end up chasing for a long time to come. The same thing Cody was chasing and still had not caught. A high like no other high. "Let's chase it together." was Cody's last thought before he too succumbed to it. The imminent danger was now secondary to the insatiable craving. And the insatiable bliss to follow. A high on Fentanyl. Like Kevin had just done, Cody sniffed away.

Cody had personally experienced as close to the biggest danger there was, taking too much and surviving it. When it happened, it seemed as if a sign that he should stop using. Yet, he ignored it and kept on. Otherwise, he knew he wouldn't be with Kevin that night. In one way or another, he would be absent. The razor's edge of dosing Fentanyl is thin and one evening not that long ago, at home with Brandi, he rode that edge too closely. He remembered finding himself stirring back to life on the floor with vomit in his mouth and a mess all about. He knew he had passed out and he knew why. While he and Brandi cleaned the carpet where he had laid just this side of death the night before he vowed to himself to never take that much again. Not a vow to stop, only a vow to get better at the dosing! "But what was too much?" he thought standing there with Kevin as the Fentanyl took hold. The pain from the new tattoos, slowly numbing. It was now becoming nonexistent under her touch. He'd learned the hard way the truth that Fentanyl was measured in micrograms not milligrams like other opiates. An amount you couldn't even see. The difference between a 'good high' and your 'last high' couldn't even be weighed on a scale. He knew that 'a life' was weighed in the balance every time she came around. This was now more than his life being weighed. It was a good thing he was high, or he might be crushed under the weight of that reality.

With the carbonation now settled in the 'Red Bull', Cody grabbed the can. Kevin grabbed his drink as well and they both sat down. Their legs were heavy, and they needed to sit. In the one minute that took to get settled, Kevin and Cody, both felt her stirring to life inside them. With Kevin's eyes now more closed than a minute prior Cody knew he was meeting her for the first time. Fentanyl. Cody remembered his first night meeting her as he sat there watching Kevin's new state emerge. The state of being controlled by her. At Jason's house months prior Cody had Googled "How much Fentanyl should you do?" It hadn't come from the supplier with any 'How to' instructions. Due to its popularity and the casualties reported in the media, Cody and Jason wanted to make sure they weren't about to make a fatal mistake that night. Newbies they were. They had figured the dosing from the internet the best they could. Yet, even with that, they knew they were rolling the dice that held their fate. They won the role, survived, and experienced the high of their life. Several nights later they had won again. His hope was to keep on winning. As he sat there next to Kevin and waited, his hope was that he had won again.

For what seemed like a long time they both just sat there lost in the high she provided. No words were needed. They would only get in the way and disrupt their beautiful experience. The ecstasy of the highest caliber. Cody sensed that Kevin was clearly experiencing something great as his head was tilted way back in his seat. Cody was tentative in searching for signs of life by asking questions. "Hey man, how are you feeling?" Cody asked. "MmmmHmmm" Kevin murmured back in response. That was all he needed to be sure Kevin hadn't slipped into oblivion. Enough to prove air was still entering his lungs. Knowing Kevin was stable, Cody began texting Brandi. This would fill the lull in time while Kevin enjoyed himself. "He'll be coming around shortly." thinking as he punched letters into his phone with his thumbs.

Cody's texting concentration was broken by the sound of a loud slurp. Kevin had found his drink and was now facing forward. "Wow," Kevin declared. "That shit's unreal". With his words slightly slurred Cody knew she was still present, however, subdued. High enough to function. A state that was very familiar to Cody. He had begun to operate in that very state quite often now. The 'functioning high' state. Not crazy high enough for anyone to notice but high enough to subside any cravings at the time. With ambition now returning, Kevin got up from his seat and went over to his computer. "Let's do one more 'quick one' Kevin demanded. Putting his phone back in his pocket Cody got up and walked over to the computer himself. "One more what?" Cody hesitantly replied. "Surely he didn't mean another hit of Fentanyl," Cody thought. "A tattoo!" Kevin eagerly replied, with his eyes glued to the screen yet again. "Let's do one more tattoo!" he continued. Envious of his ability to function that high, Cody saw it as a challenge. "No way you can tattoo right now," Cody said. "Watch me" Kevin replied.

It was actually surreal that Cody found himself once again that night in Kevin's tattoo chair. Kevin had somehow come up with just what Cody needed to get him back. Another skull. This time in-between the two skulls already on his chest. The ones Cody had inked back in college, that night after working at 'The Outback'.

Unbeknownst to Kevin, Cody had snuck another tiny bump of Fentanyl just before sitting back down. Kevin had been prepping his gun for the work and Cody used the timing wisely, so he thought. He was experiencing quite 'the high'. He was riding the razor's edge again and he knew it. As the needles pressed in and out of his skin all he could think about was sleep. Between his job, the drugs he sold, and the drugs he did, sleep was rare. "I'm ready to crash," Cody thought. With the Red Bull fading and the Fentanyl gaining strength Cody began to close his eyes as he laid there getting tattooed. His phone buzzed. Pulling it from his pocket and mustering just enough strength to open his eyes back up, he read the screen. It was his sister Kaylee. She wanted to know when he was coming home again. "Home, what's that, where's that?" Cody thought as he closed his eyes again. "Home isn't where I went to high school in Liberty or where I attended college at Northwest, is it? Those are past memories of a different home than Kaylee is asking me, isn't it? Or the people I left there too." Cody's thoughts now wandering. "It surely isn't here in Omaha, is it? It isn't in Philadelphia where Mom relocated with her new family, is it? I never lived up in Iowa where Kaylee now lived with my real Dad's family, so it couldn't be there, could it? Where really is home?" Cody continued to ponder this question with closed eyes. The hum of Kevin's gun once again acting like a hypnotist's tool. "I'll text Kaylee back tomorrow" being his last conscious thought.

Cody, now thinking he was asleep, saw himself in a dream of being incarcerated. A dream of going to prison. "Home is where I land when this thing all comes crashing down," was the last thought he remembered before passing out in Kevin's chair.

It seemed like a microsecond later that Cody found himself standing in the mirror to inspect Kevin's work, the skull was semi-complete. Always rushing onto the next tattoo before finishing the last one appeared to be a common theme with Kevin as evident by what Cody was seeing in the mirror. "Next week we'll finish everything and start the arm sleeves" Kevin promised. "Yeah man, I can't even really show them off yet, not like this. Let's get them finished ASAP" Cody replied. Rubbing ointment on the skull in the middle of his chest. Cody for the first time realized he now had 5 skulls on his body. Clearly, any omen being seen in that fact had not set in yet.

...TOO FAR I GO!

I set out for another long night of filling the orders. Making steroids was time-consuming to say the least. As I drove to Jason's condo across town, I couldn't help but recall the past weekend with Kevin. "Wild," I thought. Kevin had been continually texting me in the days that followed that 'surprise drug' tattoo session. He wanted more of the good stuff, of course. I couldn't blame him. I knew full well that she had that ability to hook you in after one measly hit. She was clearly at it now with Kevin. Exactly as she had with me. She seemed to be rearranging our entire molecular makeup so as to make us seek her, depend on her. Oxy was good at that same thing but nothing as masterful at it as Fentanyl. Kevin was now caught in the chase for her. His constant texts, proof of that. As bad as I felt for him, the pain he was probably experiencing without her, I knew I couldn't trust him with her by himself. I surely wasn't ready for that kind of responsibility.

I had experienced those same withdrawals too. With an earlier order that hadn't reached our destination as expected, I was left 'not high' and dry for days. Forced to sweat and shake until I could get my hands on her, it had been an incredibly miserable week. I had no choice but to call into work with the 'Flu'. The 'Flu?' Ha-ha, "The Flu was a joke compared to the pain I'm feeling." I remembered thinking at the time. Kevin surely wasn't experiencing anything that bad yet, I knew he was definitely hurting. "And to think, hurting only from one night," I thought as I parked my car in Jason's drive. "What really is this stuff? Why is it so addictive?" These thoughts were racing through my mind as I headed up to Jason's front door. I was eager to show off the new ink, even if it was still a work in progress. I was even more eager to snort a new bump of her.

As I climbed the stairs to the condo, I felt my phone vibrating in my pocket. Pulling it out and reading the screen, I saw it was another text from Kevin. I had used the Fentanyl as a tool to get the tattoos from Kevin without using my cash, and it had worked. Having 'some' common sense I remained apprehensive to sell any Fentanyl to Kevin. It took an extreme amount of trust for me to sell any, period. That kind of trust Kevin hadn't yet built with me. As a matter of fact, I only had one Fentanyl client and he had promised me he'd never let anyone else do it. "Do I delete Kevin's number?" I thought as I continued to climb the stairs. I knew full well that I wanted the arm sleeves to cover the Chinese symbols but debated whether it was worth it if I had to put up with Kevin's constant requests for Fentanyl. "Maybe I could push the arm sleeves up a few days and get this over with." I pondered to myself as I stepped into Jason's living room.

I immediately showed off the new ink to Jason. He never did do a good job of hiding his real opinion and his impression was mediocre at best. "Come on, they aren't even done. He still has to finish the smoke" I tried to justify the mess. The "I can't wait to see what they look like finished, man" coming from Jason's mouth only solidified his opinion. Subpar. "I'm going to head upstairs and shower really quick. Can you get everything out? I'll be down in a second." Jason was already climbing the stairs to his bedroom, talking over his shoulder at me. "Sure man" I replied.

Before I got out the equipment to make the steroids, I said to myself "First things first". I pulled a small bag of Fentanyl from my pocket and lined up a quick hit on the table. I debated briefly whether or not to grab a needle from Jason's cabinet and instead feeling pressed for time went with the quicker route. "Loading the needle would take too long" I confirmed the decision to myself. I sensed that the line I laid out looked a tiny bit bigger than my normal line, but I figured with my tolerance for her advancing I could handle it. Besides, I remembered that tonight would be a long night. "I'd need it", I concluded. Bending down with the straw I had retrieved from its familiar spot in one of the drawers I snorted the line completely. Then, sitting down on Jason's couch I waited for her to kick in. "It will only take a second," I told myself.

I wasn't thinking about dying. I never had done that. All I ever seemed to consciously care about was the present moments that existed. Sitting there on the couch I had become paralyzed, frozen in time as she grabbed me, comforted me. I laid back. Her security, a spider's web. Soon to be trapped, she began whispering words that rationalized the havoc she was soon to inflict. "Close your eyes", she whispered. I complied. Her touch, warm and soothing. All the problems that existed in my life were for an instant gone…forgotten.

I knew this kind of high had an enormous cost but as she surged through my veins it was all justified. My body, now a puppet of flesh and bone controlled by its master, Fentanyl. I needed her more than anything and now I had her. I may question friends, family, even myself, but at least I knew I had her. There was nothing more important than this high. She understood me, sympathized. She made rock bottom a place of peace, less cold and lonely. Her seeds were now planted as I could feel my eyes beginning to roll back into my head. Wondering if it was her destructive path that was slowly and methodically edging its way through my sure-to-be a lifeless body if she succeeded. Was another victim about to be thrown to the wolves? Would my pound of flesh be ravenously eaten? Would I be pulled apart with greedy chomps? I felt like I was waiting to be devoured, clueless like the lamb sent to the slaughter. My chest, no longer rising and falling with my breath. She's upon me now. Her weight, one of immovable force. I fight against her as I realize her intentions. But she's too strong for my weakened state. She wraps her long fingers around my throat and squeezes, cutting off my air like a plunge into an icy lake, Fentanyl, the Executioner. As I overdose, everything goes black. I succumb.

When I was brought back to life by the shot it felt like I had been out for only seconds. Thank God Jason had forgotten something downstairs before he jumped into the shower. He had returned to the living room to find me laying over the back of the couch like an Afghan blanket. Unresponsive, he had tried all the tricks he could muster. Pinching me, punching me, hitting me with a blast of cold water. He tried everything with no results. Finally, he knew the only thing to do was to call 911.

The paramedics had resuscitated me with Narcan, an opiate addict's guardian angel, so to speak. It kick-started my body back to life. When I woke, I sensed the paramedics and cops knew I had overdosed. But, seeing the cops, I immediately shook off my drug-induced state. I told them I had simply fallen asleep. Believing any excuse would work, I heard myself saying "I'm not sure why you guys are making such a big deal about this, as a matter of fact, why are you even here?" I attempted to debate. I would find out later that they had searched my vehicle and my person and found nothing. I had gotten lucky. My friend was a quick thinker, ridding the scene of any kind of evidence. But for the moment all I knew was they were there hovering over me and I needed them gone. I refused the ambulance ride and their constant demands that I at least, go to the hospital to be checked on. "Come on man, this is serious. We need to look you over," a familiar-looking paramedic said emphatically. "I think that I have sold steroids to this guy once before in the parking lot at the gym," my mind twisting in thought. "No thanks, I'm good. I just need a little sleep" I was quick to respond. Tired of browbeating me, they finally left me to sort it all out myself.

With all that so fresh in my mind, I began to form a new outlook on life. However, that new look once again didn't include me putting a stop to making steroids. Or for that matter, a stop to using them or fentanyl. For now, I would frame the wake-up call of the overdose as less about stopping anything and more about my need to get a lot better at managing everything, especially dosing.

My close friends that knew what happened would ask my opinion on the subject, my take on surviving an overdose. "I'm more appreciative than ever to be alive" I'd say knowing I was lying to them and myself. No real improvements would be made. Just words said to cover lies. I felt I had an image to uphold, a position to maintain, and people depended on me. Importance. Power. Money. Strength. Status. All were the makeup of my persona. At least that is what I told myself to support my lack of change. Yet, the other voice that worked to push it away said it was really all a lie. But "How would people view me if they knew I was an addict? Weak!" I thought. So, I told them exactly what they wanted to hear, and I needed to hear more. Lies that despite all the mess I was in, I continued to allow to be spoken to myself to assure me that everything was just fine. That I was just fine.

It all worked so well that the night after I had overdosed, I wouldn't go to bed without snorting another line. It seemed that for some reason I just didn't care.

7

THE EXECUTIONER'S VOICE

...TOO MUCH

If God had bigger plans for Cody, he hadn't yet uncovered them. Cody was turning over the wrong stones or wasn't interested in looking at all. He hadn't slowed down in the least, quite the opposite. The overdose had woken him up for a few days, however, the experience was only life-changing until he couldn't contend with the mounting withdrawals. Now caught between those stones he felt their weight crushing him. Just the mental exercise of thinking of the work it would take for change seemed insurmountable to him. So, the horrific experience wouldn't be life-changing at all even though he had prayed right after the ordeal and in the following days. "Thank you, God, for saving my life," is all he could repeat. Now, even that prayer began fading. Time had once again numbed the experience, like anything tragic, it was impactful, then not. Taking the path of least resistance, or no resistance at all, he had reverted easily back to his old ways, full steam ahead! All the overdose did was open his eyes to 'how' irresponsibly he had been in using. It had more or less simply educated him on his drug-taking habits. If anything, he told himself, "I can't snort this stuff anymore. It's too messy and not precise enough." Cody had started by just dabbling with injecting Fentanyl but now that had become the only way, he used it. He thought he had developed a fail-proof strategy, inject the powder he would normally snort but in two sessions, not one. One push of the plunger, injecting only half of the drug. Then wait until he was certain the drug had climaxed, then inject the other half. He didn't think he could go wrong with such a strategy. Believing, by doing it in that way she couldn't get too close to him. Cody didn't want to meet her again in the same fashion he had on Jason's couch. Not because he was scared of dying, that fear had now worn off. But he didn't want to have to explain himself to his friends, including Jason, so he only offered up, "It was just an accident man, chill out, it won't happen again."

Not only was Cody now injecting Fentanyl regularly, but Brandi was gone too. Foolishly, Cody had screwed that up too by leaving his phone unguarded within her reach. Brandi had secretly gone through his phone one night to find provocative pictures of other women, lots of them. Cody had become lazy and forgotten to delete his messages before coming home that night. He was slipping in his 'ruse' and it had become evident by his inability to pull off the maneuvers he once did. Park Car. Delete Texts. Enter the house. Safe. 'Being the player, 101' wasn't as easy as it once had been. Thinking he had once written the rulebook on it; Cody now had a hard time executing elementary plays. Smooth no more, it was now over, no more plays needed.

"Pack your bags and leave then. Good luck finding anyone who'll take care of you like I do." Cody's bravado argued the morning after she found the pictures. She didn't believe his tale and simply left after he took off for work. She made off with about five grand and a

TV. When he arrived home to find the money and TV stolen Cody wasn't surprised. "Keep it" he had thought to himself. "What can I do anyway, report it, bringing the heat on me?" he continued. He laughed that evening as he purchased a new TV at Wal-Mart. A bigger 72 inch this time, of course, he knew he would have new women to impress.

Brandi's place became easily filled. Different women rotated between the nights filling Steroid orders with Jason. With the operation now moved into Cody's house, at least he didn't have to drive across town to Jason's' condo. Sometimes, if it weren't too late after filling the orders, Cody could have a girl over that same night. With all the new women in Cody's life, it didn't surprise him when a once special woman from his past resurfaced among them. Lauren.

Yet, the reason she had come over was as a friend to help Cody clean his house up after she found out Brandi had left him. Cody knew he needed some sort of fresh start and Lauren was more than willing to help. She opened the windows and pulled the curtains back to a gloomy mess. "You. Have. Got. To. Be. Kidding. Me?!" she said as the light hit the living room floor. The place was a disaster. With Lauren standing in the sun Cody wasn't sure what he was seeing as he squinted into the light. The rays of sun beaming around her figure. It felt good, both the sun and Lauren's presence. Warm and comfortable. But they were currently feelings of appreciate that he didn't want a woman giving him. Feelings he realized and seemed to accept he was seeking in his drugs, not people. "Why does she still care about me after all I've done to her?" Cody asked himself as he helped clean up. While Lauren was upstairs Cody snuck into the bathroom to shoot some Fentanyl. "Subdue it. Bury it. Run."

he thought as he looked into the mirror, bags under his sleepy eyes. "I'm a wreck," evident from his reflection. "No wonder she's concerned," he thought. They made small talk while cleaning. All questions from her regarding his current lifestyle choices were rerouted or dodged completely. Anything but the truth remained satisfactory enough for him.

When they finished the cleanup Cody quickly ushered her to the door. "Thanks for helping Lauren, I appreciate it," he said, looking towards the floor. Demanding eye contact, she turned abruptly and pulled his chin up, and looked straight into Cody's eyes. She became serious much like he remembered she once had when she asked Cody to move to Omaha with her a few years back. Yet she wasn't now asking Cody to start a new life with her as she had in college. Cody was now a man that was a galaxy much further away than he had been in those days. Lauren was curious about the life he was living. One she struggled to recognize as if wondering "Is this the same guy I last saw when I drove out of his life?" He sensed that at best she saw him as one word, 'dark'. Then she confirmed it and spoke, "Where's the old Cody? The one that laughed constantly and made everyone around him smile? Talk to me. Something's going on. You're a mess. Besides, how the hell can you afford all this stuff working at Boys Town?" "Lie to her!" Cody instantly thought. "Do what you do best and lie," he continued. So, he did, "I'm better than ever Lauren, I got a promotion and work a ton of extra hours. They need me there." Continuing the utterance of lies, "I'm just tired, that's all". He knew she knew well enough that he wasn't telling her the truth. Yet, as she stepped down Cody's front stairs she turned and said, "Well, I'm here for you if you need me," and walked away. This time Cody watched her drive away instead of the other way around.

Despite having lots of friends and money, Cody at that very moment felt lonely. This was something that was no longer being salved by dollar bills, vodka, and the continual mental subduing by Fentanyl. His use of it was increasing. He didn't feel the need to impress people anymore and became more of an isolated creature. Depressed, Cody began praying at home, asking God for help. "Why did you save me? I'm nothing but a junkie. What is your purpose for me?" Cody found himself high and now begging God for his help. However, the answers he asked never seemed to be answered. This drug that was now empowering Cody was pretty good at drowning out any sort of Godly voice. Not that he was searching all that hard anyway. Any voice God was whispering sure wasn't being received. Cody would just chalk it up as another unanswered prayer.

One night with yet another new girl, Cody flipped through the movies on Netflix, searching for anything to watch. The movie choice didn't matter. The presence of continual groping was his non-verbal to hurry up and pick something. Anything. "Funny or Scary?" he asked. As he scrolled with the remote his cut-off shirt revealed one of the Chinese tattoos. "Scary" she spouted out. He didn't know if she meant the tattoo or the movie as she was look-ing at his right arm. "Hey, what does that mean?" she continued. Already convinced the symbol was ridiculous Cody immediately went into his defense mode. "Dumb huh, it means Faith," he mut-tered still looking at the TV, afraid to make eye contact with her. "I'm just looking for the right tattoo guy to get them covered. My last artist got locked up. I still need to finish all this too." Cody said lifting his shirt, now showing off the almost finished skulls.

Finally picking a scary movie on Netflix, Cody put the remote back down and now fully removed his shirt. "If tattoos are what she wants to see, tattoos are what I'll show her." Cody thought.

With his shirt now off and the movie starting in the background she decided to pull her long sleeves up on her shirt. Conspicuous at first, Cody didn't know what she was doing. Then, the famous MGM Lion appeared with its signature roaring face staring back. She next revealed a collage of tattoos on her forearm including a skull collage of her own. Cody felt a twinge of excitement inside him as he looked over in awe eying the numerous skulls on her body. "Do you like it?", she said. "Like it?" Cody yelled. "I love it!" He was now connected to this stranger through the love of skull tattoos and soon hopefully the connection of sex. "I guess we have something in common." she laughed. "I guess we do, don't we?" Cody said smiling back. "Want to see another one? " she asked. Now standing and still smiling she then pulled up 'her' shirt to her pelvis area revealing another skull. "Nice," Cody said. He was trying to contain his excitement. This had somehow turned into a skull 'Show & Tell'. "How much further would this go?" Cody wondered as a scream in the movie was echoing in the room.

"You should go to my artist. He'll finish those skulls and cover that Chinese symbol for you. He did my skulls, he's awesome at them," she offered while sitting and pulling her shirt back down. "Actually, I got two Chinese symbols" Cody replied, turning to show her the other triceps ink. "Ahh, the Chinese symbol phase. I got a little secret for you." she giggled. Bending over and lowering her sock she revealed a Chinese symbol on her ankle. Cody was now ecstatic with the thought that God himself must have sent this girl. He couldn't help but yell "No Way!?" "It means 'Strength'" she said pulling her sock back into place. "What does your other one mean?" She asked. "Courage" he replied. "Faith on the right arm and courage on the left. Like I said though, I'd really like to get them covered. It's quite funny that you have a skull collage on your arm. That's exactly what I was thinking of getting to cover my symbols up." She jumped in, "Here let me give you the number to my artist, I'll let him know you're going to text him."

Now sitting back on the couch with this newly connected girl in his arms Cody grabbed his phone from his pocket and they exchanged numbers. Cody couldn't help but laugh "A tattoo artist on speed dial," he thought to himself as he entered the number. They both decided it was best to now watch the movie, if only for a moment.

...TOO DEEP

With the tattoos being only semi-finished on his torso, Cody hated seeing them every day in his mirror. "Hideous." he thought now staring at himself shirtless. He had contemplated texting the artist Autumn had given him, wanting to call several times in the following weeks but never quite finding enough time. As he continued looking at the tattoos he simultaneously reached into his pocket for his phone. Holding the hard plastic, he thumbed the smooth screen not yet looking down. An indecisive mannerism. Debating. "I do have a free Saturday tomorrow," thinking to himself. "Maybe I could get one of my sides done." he continued. He decided to get the skulls Kevin hadn't yet completed done another time. Cody still couldn't believe Kevin had gotten himself into so much trouble. The last he had heard Kevin had been pulled over for possession of some pills. Their tattoo ideas could wait, right now, Cody wanted something brand new. As he continued mulling all this, his phone buzzed. Looking down at the screen he saw it was another female. This caused him to ignore for a second the loaded syringe of Fentanyl lying on the counter below the mirror. His mind now moved into another realm.

Cody had been building resentment towards women and he knew it. He seemed to be convincing himself time and time again that they would always leave. Even though he knew he was the catalyst to his failed relationships, he still blamed them for the pain of it. "Did all this relationship 'crap' come from my high school sweetheart leaving me in my senior year after having an abortion? Or from my mother, who had moved to Philadelphia as soon as I went off to college? Hell, I've only seen her a handful of times in the last decade. Maybe it's from the time I discovered that my 2-year college girlfriend had cheated on me with more than one football guy! Whatever the case, I hate women. All of them!" all this swirling through his head as he stared between himself in the mirror and the buzzing phone. Continuing, "Every time I get close to them, they leave. Every time I opened myself up to them, it is all for nothing. The women I rarely seem to connect with, I only find out later that they feel the same way I do when it comes to the men in their life. Even about me! So, we find ourselves coming to a mutual understanding, a purely physical one." Cody knew the biggest challenge wasn't really the leaving part of the relationship, it was what came afterward. Once they left, every time they left, he would fill the awful feeling of the 'no love' void with the wonderful feeling of his 'real love'. The synthetic, man-made kind of love. Love like the one laying right in front of him on the counter. And he knew this day the cycle would once again continue.

Autumn, like Lauren and Brandi before her had eventually gotten fed up with Cody. He once again had found a way to implode the small resemblance of a personal relationship. She had gotten too close for Cody's comfort and she had been soon placed on the back burner of his life; Cody's place for females who began to explore him in depths too deep. Autumn, of course, didn't enjoy this one bit and decided to move on. Again, it seemed that women like Autumn were hard for Cody to understand. "Why do they have a compelling need to move into trying to understand me?" Cody questioned. "Too many feelings. Too many emotions for me." he continued. He would rather his women remain more surface, more physical. Moving from women to women Cody was attempting to have the benefits of companionship yet keep them just out of emotional reach. A comfort zone Cody seemed to prefer with women. "It's not like they wouldn't leave anyway?" the old thoughts resurfaced. "Why give them the satisfaction of getting too close." Cody was trying to hold true to the age-old motto "Leave them before they leave you!" Yet, it was becoming quite obvious that they were now the ones really leaving first!

Several more women would enter and leave Cody's life after Autumn. All but one would remain true and would not leave him, his beloved Fentanyl. She knew everything about Cody and Cody didn't seem to mind.

"Why am I even messing with these other women anyway?" he thought. "They don't understand me, and they never will." he continued. Finally, he assured himself that for certain 'love' was a pipe dream. So, with that, Cody slowly began giving up on having girls over altogether. He instead would come home from work and make steroids with Jason at his kitchen table. Most of the time high, usually capping off the night with another shot of her and a movie by himself. He would wake up alone the next day and go to work at Boys Town then do it all over again the next night. It had become a routine. With the overdose getting further and further in the rearview mirror of his life, Cody began pushing the envelope of dosing amounts of intake again. Testing the limits of his tolerance, always aiming for that elusive better high. His fail-proof strategy of injecting seemed no longer needed. "I am fully experienced now." he convinced himself when he was looking down at that fresh needle. He had also convinced himself an overdose 'couldn't' possibly happen again, something that 'wouldn't' happen again. He wasn't going to let it.

"That's what I'll get for my new tattoo!" his mind trying to switch back to his current tattoo mission. Yet, holding his unanswered phone in his hand and leaving the message box he'd just opened; he tried to ignore the girl attempting to make plans. Instead hearing the voice of the Fentanyl, she offered, "This will be something to represent the women in my life. Sexy and deadly. Elusive and free. This will be something to represent them completely." Cody looked again down at the needle on the counter and allowed her to convince him that "This will represent all of them that have taken a piece of me. All of them that continue to hurt me." With that he picked up the needle.

Leaving the bathroom and plopping down on the couch Cody visualized the first image of the new tattoo he was creating in his mind; an image of a beautiful woman came alive. His phone now sitting on the coffee table, he sat back enjoying the high. Again, the tattoo he envisioned, a beautiful woman. She was a combination of all the females Cody had used. He pictured her fully as he now laid back and closed his eyes. She was holding something too, a smoking gun. An always visible representation of the overdose. A symbol of the aftershock of what a bullet could do, what she could do, bring pain. She had a tattoo herself. A tattoo on the tattoo. A rose was placed delicately on her breast. The rose, a representation to her of what she represents to Cody; something you could never quite grab unless you were willing to subject yourself to an inherent amount of risk. The risk of the high of love. A high like no other. The same things that she and Cody would chase. "Could you have it without hurt?" Cody thought. Of course, she'd have a face tattoo on her as well. Something Cody hadn't yet been bold enough to get. She was tougher than him though. More man than Cody could ever be. If Russian roulette was an image, she was it. Cody sat up and grabbed his phone. He began texting Juan; the artist Autumn had given him. He now knew exactly what he wanted, he wanted her.

It just so happened that Juan had an available slot the next day. Cody was more than happy to fill it. They chatted on the phone about the image Cody envisioned. The female he wanted on his right rib cage. "I can have it drawn up for you and ready by the time you come in," Juan said. They also discussed Kevin and his unfinished work, the skulls on Cody's torso. "If we get enough time, we can finish those too." Juan continued. Cody was ecstatic to begin the work, eager for more tattoos. "Oh, and by the way, I have these

symbols on my arms that I'm going to eventually need to have covered up too. I was thinking larger versions of the skull collage you
did on Autumn," Cody offered. "Symbols?" Juan replied, curious
about what Cody meant. "Just some dumb Chinese symbols on my
triceps. They mean Faith and Courage" Cody replied. "Slow down.
We can get that taken care of too. Let's get this girl done first" Juan
suggested, just as eager as Cody to get going. After hanging up the
phone he thought about the pain he was about to endure. Knowing
it would be about a four-hour tattoo session in one of the most
painful areas on the body, he smiled, as if welcoming it. "Oh well,
I've got just the thing to make it bearable." He knew he'd have to
arrive prepared. He'd have to have a couple of needles loaded in his
car, "or should I just bring a little power and hit a key bump in the
bathroom?" Cody mulled his plan. His drug use was now becoming
riskier by the day. He opted out of driving with that raw powder on
him and continued with plan A – injecting as this wouldn't be like
Kevin's shop. He sensed it would be more mainstream and the drug
use inside wouldn't be permitted. "That's ok," he thought, "I'll just
have to take a couple of breaks to the car. Since when has hiding my
use been an issue? No reason to let it start being one now."

Cody pulled up to the location of the shop the following day in his
maroon Chrysler. It was already dark out. The bustling crowds on the
streets, oblivious to the needle Cody was putting in his arm. "They
can't see inside the tinted windows." Cody thought. "Even in the
daytime." Pulling out the needle and sitting back in the soft leather
seats he had his hands gripped on the steering wheel. Cody waited
for her to come to life in him. On cue and on time she did. "There
you are." Cody thought, releasing his grip from the wheel, color now

returning to his knuckles. He opened the door to his car and stepped into the night air, now absolutely ready to get another tattoo.

They shook hands and introduced themselves to one another. "I'm going to go get everything ready, go ahead and take a seat over there," Juan said to Cody pointing to a chair in the far corner of the shop. The place was huge. The ceiling, at least 20 ft high, the shop occupying a couple of floors of an old, restored warehouse. Tattoo images were scaling the walls as far up as you could see. High on Fentanyl, he took a seat in the instructed chair after walking past two Harley Davidson motorcycles parked in the middle of the shop. Hispanic music was blaring in the background. The building was located in the southern area of Omaha. The Hispanic district. Most of the tattoos on the walls had a touch of Hispanic culture in the artwork. One wall was dedicated solely to Hispanic tattoo images of Mother Mary and Jesus. A bit of Catholicism was also infused into tattoo culture. While Juan was off getting his tattoo gun ready Cody continued to take in the vastness of tattoo art options. He soon recognized one of the pictures about halfway up a wall. The picture was of Jesus wearing his crown of thorns. The same picture he had seen on the calendar in his Boys Town office. Cody and Jesus again stared at each other for what seemed to him like an eternity, as if oblivious to the other tattoo guns buzzing and the music blaring. The other people coming and going into the shop, all unnoticed in this surreal moment as Cody gulped down the spit in his throat. He could have heard a needle drop through the noise. Time froze as he stared at the picture of Jesus. Cody at once gathered himself and turned away. Juan was calling his name, walking in his direction. "Hey man, you ready to get rolling?" Juan eagerly said, bringing Cody back to the reality of where he was and why he was there. Tattoo time.

Just as he lay there in Juan's tattoo chair facing the montage of religious graffiti, he was certain he was hearing a voice. Juan fired up the tattoo gun. A buzzing familiar to Cody. Both hypnotic and fearful, Cody could feel the pain of the needle before contact with his skin was made. Like a splitting headache in football just before his helmet made contact with the opponent. His brain and nerves assimilating the sound of the buzzing gun to the feeling of his previous tattoos. That voice somewhere behind it all. That voice Cody couldn't yet understand.

Now that he was laying on his side getting tattooed it put the art on the wall right in Cody's line of view. The picture of Jesus wearing the crown was soon looking down at him. Cody's face became twisted in agony, the Fentanyl seeming to rapidly wear off. "Don't go to your car and inject the poison?" the voice in Cody's head said. With the outline done, Juan got up from his seat. "I'm going to grab a drink; I'll be right back," Juan said. An opportune time to go to his car, Cody continued hearing the voice. "You're strong, you can handle it." the voice continued. "But I'm not, I'm weak. I need it." Cody pushing back, working to convince the voice. Cody struggled with these thoughts, these dueling voices. Fighting the urge Cody remained in the chair laying on his side. The voice reminded Cody of his mother's when he was younger. "You don't need this stuff" she had said after his elbow injury. Despite his mother, who he hadn't seen for five years now, He decided to stay in the chair. He wanted to prove to somebody or something he could take it, the pain without the assistance of Fentanyl.

A few hours later the tattoo was done. Cody stood in the mirror inspecting the work. He was moving from side to side with one arm

over his head, smiling. With his other arm, he began rubbing ointment on the fresh tattoo. It was exactly what he envisioned. "Man,
that hurt" Cody said. "You made it through" Juan replied standing
next to Cody, arm's crossed. Looking upon another satisfied client.
"Let's meet up again in a few weeks and start working on that skull
collage," Cody said as he handed Juan a wad of cash while thinking it was surely enough to cover the tattoo." "Sounds like a plan
Cody." Juan agreed as he took it.

On the drive back home Cody was contemplating whether or not
to inject the already pre-loaded needles of Fentanyl sitting next to
him. Normally he would have hit it by now but the voice from the
shop was still echoing through his head saying, "You don't need this
stuff" For a few minutes he believed it. Believing whatever that voice
was in his head. He felt something impelling him to believe it. A
motivation he hadn't known or felt for years. One that he started to
think was coming from the deficiency of drugs in his system.   An
internal drive to rise from this mess.

For a minute he felt like quitting as the voice put in his head, "I
should call someone and tell them everything. Lauren? Mom? or
Dad? Anyone!" He scrolled to his mom's number on his phone.
His thumb millimeters above the screen, he could almost feel the
smooth plastic. Yet, an impenetrable force field between his thumb
and the screen remained.

Right then, he had the powerful urge to blow the whistle on himself. With that Cody instantly began to cry from the madness of
knowing that he couldn't do it. "I can't tell on myself, can I? I can't
admit my drug habit to my family, can I? I can't admit these types of
failings to them, can I? Wait, what's up with this relentless picture

of Jesus wearing the crown of thorns I'm still seeing anyway?" Cody began pressing somebody with the image still being seen in his conscious eye. He pulled into his driveway and putting his car into park he now looked down at his phone. With tears still in his eyes and headlights beaming off his garage, it created a holographic glow of lights in his eyes. He went from contacts to Google and typed into the search bar 'Jesus and thorns'. Cody hit the first link he could and wiped the tears from his eyes. As it popped up Cody began reading. Matthew 13:5-9. "And some fell among thorns, and the thorns sprang up and choked them. But others fell on good ground and yielded a crop: some a hundredfold, some sixty, some thirty. He who has ears to hear, let him hear." The scripture quoted from Jesus himself. Cody set his phone down next to the needles. The thorns. The voice. The scripture. "Simply a coincidence." Cody surmised. He then picked the needle up, closing off the voice, ignoring what he heard. Sticking the needle into his arm he injected half the drug. "Simply a coincidence" he continued thinking as he sat back and let the drug engulf him as he again white-knuckled the steering wheel.

...TOO FAR, AGAIN!

"Let everyone know your dirty little secret" it had begun, the voice in my head. I knew my body was craving the drug. I texted the girl back and set my phone on the kitchen counter. The prospects of a movie with someone new were floating through my head. Something or someone to take my mind off everything for a while. "Just come in when you get here." my text began, "The front door is unlocked for you." my thumbs continued. Just then I could feel the new tattoo under my dress shirt, the collared polo I wore to work that day. The scabs occasionally being pulled by the nylon fabric of the shirt. I wanted throughout the day to pick them off, but I had so far fought the urge successfully. "Let it heal!" I told myself. As I carefully pulled the shirt off, I heard that earlier voice returns to my head saying "Call your mom and dad. Let them know what you're about to do". I set the shirt on the counter shaking my head. A sickness in my stomach began to bubble. I cold paleness on my skin. But here I stood sweating. "What are you going to do now?" the voice teased. "Shut up!" I heard myself say. I stood in my kitchen, just me, and this voice. I reached up into one of my familiar cabinets and grabbed a baggie of white powder. Greedily, I sprinkled a copious amount on the counter. "Instead of taking the time to prepare a needle, I will do just a little bump first. If I snort this really quick, it will at least take the edge off and quiet this nagging voice in my head." I retrieved a credit card from my wallet.

Ever since putting the tattoo of her on my side, I seemed to be continually battling two powerful opposing things: One voice pushing me to tell someone I needed help and stop this destructive path, and another voice of hunger telling me to get high and continue. Not a want to get high but a hunger. Something much deeper than a want. The urge would always win out. The urge to get high. "Who wanted an intervention anyway?" I thought. Although insistent, the 'tell someone' voice hadn't won. Hadn't even really come close. Matter of fact, getting high was the only thing that quieted the battling voices. It now seemed in my head to be a double-edged sword, as if it were actually the same voice saying two opposing things. When I'd feel the itch to hit the Fentanyl, the battling of the voice was at its loudest. Almost annoying. Guaranteeing that injecting was the only thing that shut the battling up. It's like the single voice knew I wouldn't listen to the 'get help' directive. It knew in fact that I would soon get high to quiet it. It was as if I had discovered this reverse psychology tactic from that clever voice now at play. It would tell me to tell on myself, knowing that I wouldn't. It was while pondering its cleverness, that I recognized the voice for what it was. At that very moment I knew I was in deep shit. I recognized that the cleverness of the hunger's voice had been winning all along, not me. I felt I was graduating. Not like with the college degree I had worked so hard to receive a few years earlier. This was a much darker graduation. I was graduating from user to an addict. From addict to Junkie. From junkie to possessed. All of the reality of it came rushing together at that very moment in my kitchen.

It was now suffocating me, and it needed it to be quieted as soon as possible. I was right all along, there was "no time to load the needle." I pulled a sliver-sized line from the pile. The credit card making a couple of quick 'chop chops' against the granite countertop. I was in a bad spot and needed it now! I never thought my life would have ever come to this. "But what drug fiend does?" I thought, staring at the line that was staring back at me. Neither blinking. Fixated on the microscopic crystals of Fentanyl. My life was becoming a series of snapshots speeding through my head, from current to past. I reached the beginning. My thoughts stop, I'm a child, innocent and free. Running with my two sisters in the backyard of my grandma's house. My Grandpa had built a swing set there and we always tried to see who could swing the highest. My shirt was off, soaking up the Midwestern sun. No tattoos, just clean, ink-free skin. The voice brings me back to the line in the kitchen. It's calling me to what I feel is true. I'm weak. I look at the line one last time knowing its size is iffy at best. Risky? Yes. Do I care? I should but don't! I snort it and stand up from the counter still holding my nostril as I let her consume me. I'm brought back to the present. I look down and see the smoking gun – the scabbed-over tattoo Juan had drawn the prior week. Then…nothingness.

Cody found himself waking in what appeared to be an Emergency Room. Shirtless and still in his dress pants. The ones he'd worn to work. Beep. Beep. Beep. Equipment that made noises filled the background. Equipment that assured Doctors and Nurses his heart was still working. A couple of people in white lab coats were standing over Cody as his vision cleared. He slowly understood the magnitude of his situation. "You're lucky to be alive," one of them said. He knew he had been there before, arriving that time from Jason's' living room. The questions. The accusations and funny looks. Cody shot up realizing the cops would surely be on their way if they were not already there. He began sliding his feet off the bed. He knew he had to get out of there and fast. "Unplug me!" Cody barked at the doctors. "Whoa! That's not a good idea. We need to assess you first, run some tests." A doctor forcefully replied. "Not on me you're not. Unplug me or I will do it myself." Cody began demanding. Annoyed the doctors began meeting Cody's requests. A Nurse soon showed up and shoved a waiver in his face. "Sign it if you are refusing medical treatment," she said. Cody quickly scribbled something across the paper. "Move, move, move!" he thought.

With the IV now removed Cody threw his feet on the floor and spun around to assess the environment. "If I have to, I'll walk home shirtless," Cody told himself. "It's only a few blocks." he continued. Then, he turned, and to his surprise, he met her eyes. He froze for a second. Running from one set of Doctor questions he felt as if he were now about to dive into another, more personal line of them. In the corner, there she sat. "The girl", Cody deduced "who had saved my life. The one I had told to 'Just come in when you get here, the front door is unlocked for you'." He didn't know who she was. They had only just met a couple of days prior on an online dating site. Yet, she was another 'Guardian Angel' sent into his life. One he wasn't sure he was even thankful for. "I'm sure she got more than she bargained for." Cody thought as he walked toward her.

She handed Cody his shirt. "She must have grabbed it off the counter." Cody thought. "I followed the ambulance here; I thought you might want a ride home." she said. "Are you sure you don't need to get checked out?" she continued. "I'm good, let's get out of here," Cody said pulling his shirt over his head and making sure the cops weren't around the corner.

She drove him back to his home and they hugged each other goodbye in the driveway. It was late. She had things to do the next day. Cody would probably never see her again. "It's not the first and definitely not the last." Cody mused as he walked towards his front door. He wasn't sure if he had just thought about overdoses or females in general. But it crossed his mind that it could be either, or both, nonetheless. As Cody pulled open the front door he wondered if he could even remember her name without getting his phone out. The Guardian Angel, the girl that had saved his life. He didn't even know her name.

As he walked into his kitchen, he recognized something he'd seen before. A scene wiped of evidence. "Good girl," he thought. "But where did she put it," he said to himself as he began ripping open cabinets. Finally, he found it. He threw the baggie on the counter in the same spot it had sat a few hours previous. Cody looked at it like the thing it was. Cody couldn't stand what it "was" doing to him, or what it "had" done to him. And then, he felt the urge. The Itch. A bead of sweat formed on his brow. Then he heard a voice. Just a whisper at first then slowly growing more present. Louder. "Heck of a way to get attention, Cody. You can just call them. Call your family. Anyone. They'll come to help you right now". Cody got a needle out of the cabinet.

This time he'd be smart enough to inject it.

8

THE SEARCH FOR EQUILIBRIUM...

...WITH-IN THE FAMILY

"Slow down Cody," Grandma yelled from across her backyard. I knew from the distance of her voice that she was doing chores in the garden, probably picking some vegetables for our lunch. I had just pulled myself up out of the water and was sprinting across the deck. No matter what Grandma was doing, she always seemed to know when I was running on that wet deck. A sixth sense of sorts. I slowed to a trot then down to speed walking toward my sisters on the swing set, the dry grass now crunching between my bare toes. It was common for me to need some throttling back when I was at Grandmas, I loved it here. I typically only had one speed at her house, fast. Especially now that I could swim on my own without her right there in the water with me. "All you need is a little Faith and Courage Cody," Grandma was always saying while cheering me on to swim. I trusted her and her coaching abilities and they were working. No longer using arm floaters, I was swimming solo. I was now a fish, thanks to Grandma. I was swimming just like a Ninja Turtle, pretty close to the entire length of the pool in one breath. These accomplishments in the water, they all felt so good. One of the best feelings I've ever experienced in my short life was showing my Grandma I could swim on my own. The feeling that came with her cheering voice. She would pick me up in the pool and we'd laughed together. Everything about her showed she was proud of me and I felt nothing could ever top that feeling. Just then, I joined my sisters on the swing and began pumping my legs to go higher and higher. Grandma was the one who had taught me to do that too.

I just loved it up here in Iowa. My stepmom, Deb would drop my sisters and me off for the day at Grandmas while she and my real Dad went off to work. We were only able to come to visit on holidays and sporadic weekends, but it was surely better than not being able to come at all. For me, it was a break from the chaos I felt I lived in back home with my mom and stepdad Bill. They seemed to fight a lot, and that bothered me. So, as I pumped my legs to go higher and higher on the swing, the tension from back home didn't exist. As a matter of fact, up in Iowa, whether I was at Dad's or Grandmas the anxiety of a looming heated argument wasn't there. As the wind rushed past my face and I could see my sisters laughing, I felt free. I felt like a different kid. A kid whose feelings I couldn't associate with around Bill back home. The only thing I associated with Bill was arguments. Yelling. Fighting. These things made me feel not so much like a kid. "Kids aren't supposed to be scared of someone. Are they?" I thought often. Nobody scared me here in Iowa. Not at Grandmas or Dads. That type of hostility didn't seem to exist here. Nor did the constant competition that also existed back home. I wasn't sure if Bill was pushing me so hard athletically to prove something to himself or to make me better, or both. Regardless, nobody here pushed me like that. I found myself having to consciously dial myself back when I was here. It took me a bit of time to realize Bill wasn't here and that the life of competition wasn't either. I stopped pumping to purposely let my sisters go higher than me. This was a contest I wasn't ashamed of losing. If it were instead Bill swinging with me, I would have gone all the way around the swing set just to beat him. But Grandma's house was a vacation from all that win-lose stuff.

"I'll go get some popsicles," I yelled as I jumped off the swing. "After we eat lunch, Cody!" Grandma instantly yelled back as she was walking towards the house. Carrying a bowl of green beans from the garden she continued "How about you three help me snap these beans?" Hot on Grandma's heels we followed her into the kitchen eager to help with lunch. I would not forget those popsicles though, making a mental note to search them out later. Grandma kept a freezer in the basement stocked up with them for when we came home, she would always tease us upon arrival. "Home?" I'd think when I heard it. "Where exactly was 'Home'?" I continued thinking about it once again as I entered the kitchen. "I suppose I have two homes," finally surmising but I was looking forward to too much fun to dig for deeper meaning just then.

As my sisters and I snapped the green beans Grandma flipped the grilled cheese sandwiches. Nothing beats lunch at Grandma's. The summer salads were made with fresh vegetables. Sometimes Grandma would let me dig up potatoes for her potato salad. I'd run out to the garden and plunge the pitchfork into the dirt pulling out the hidden treasures. I took satisfaction in the food I'd help make at Grandmas. Pretty soon the plates would be ready, and I'd be sitting with my sisters out back under the big umbrella on the deck, swiveling back and forth with cheeks full of food. A smile was on my face bigger than the Iowa sun. "This is the life," I thought as I continued snapping the green beans. The bad ends of the beans were put in the recycling bowl where all the other food scraps went. Grandpa would then feed them to the hogs and other animals. We continued this process until the entire bowl of beans Grandma had picked was done. The finished job and 'grilled cheese time' seemed to always meet perfectly as Grandma called, "Let's eat!"

"Make sure you wait thirty minutes before you get in the pool," Grandma said as she cleaned up the lunch mess. I was already running to the basement for the preplanned dessert. This was my cue to get my sisters and me the fudge popsicles from the freezer. As I came back up from the basement and met my sisters on the deck, I noticed Grandma had moved out to the clothesline. She was always working on some chore or another.

As I enjoyed my popsicle, I couldn't help but daydream about my upcoming departure from Grandma's. I thought about my goodbye to Grandpa. Late in the afternoon, I'd get the feeling that it wouldn't be long before Grandpa would be in for the day and Deb would shortly thereafter be back to pick us up. The fun at the farm would come to an end.

Grandpa had the same perfect timing as Grandma. He always showed up just before we left for the day. Dirty and covered in some sort of grease, he'd always be there. I'd initiate an attempt at a goodbye, shoving forward a leery and jittery hand, toward the towering presence in front of me. He was intimidating to me, but not in the same way that Bill was. "Surely this was as close as a man could get to being a god to me." I thought. Like the God I learned about in church on Wednesday nights with my sisters. The Almighty. Grandpa. The peace I felt here had been created by this man soon to be towering in front of me. "God lived in Heaven and this place was surely as close as I could get to Heaven," I continued thinking. "So surely Grandpa is Godlike," I continued. My preadolescent brain unable to differentiate Grandpa from God. I was associating comparison with my emotions. Grandpa would never accept the handshake though. He'd put his arms out inviting me in for a hug. I'd waddle forward and press my face into his dirty bib overalls covered in the mysterious grease. He'd smell like dirt and oil and everything a farmer might, like the outside, like the farm. Then he'd wrap his giant arms around me and squeeze. The man loved to hug, something Bill never did. The hug. The last thing that would solidify a day spent at Grandmas. It was soon approaching. I thought of the only thing I might do to prolong it. I ran back to the basement for more popsicles.

The day was soon to get even better than even popsicles. My Dad had gotten off work and came to pick me up to go fishing, something we both loved to do together. The goodbye with Grandpa had happened a bit earlier but just like I'd replayed it in my head under the umbrella. I looked down at the small grease smudge still on my chest from the goodbye with Grandpa. The hug.

I was now following my Dad heel to toe with my fishing pole in hand. We were headed to one of my Dad's favorite spots. One of 'our' favorite spots. I thought about the levels of the world I was in. I knew grandpa was my Dad's Dad, "But if Grandpa was godlike then Dad was just about the same," I thought this while still hot on my Dad's heels. A demi-God perhaps. All the things a Dad could teach a son about the Great Outdoors my Dad was teaching me. Fishing, hunting, camping, and even how to clean animals. When I wasn't at Grandma's, I loved doing what I was now doing, getting close to my Dad. He and I never stayed inside for long. Only bad weather ever kept us cooped up. If that did happen, we would find ourselves watching old Westerns until the rain would pass. The wilderness seemed like our personal playground.

Dad also showed me how to help others. A type of coaching I hadn't fully grasped yet. He showed me by letting me see him doing it. Dad was the best coach at helping people. Whatever task needed to be done, he seemed always right there in the middle helping in the small community where he lived. His current task though was helping me bait the darn hook. I could never get the worm on as he could, but he had the patience to show me how, time and time again. To coach me along. He wouldn't yell at me if I got it wrong. He'd simply instruct me, wait for me, correct me, and repeat the process as long as it would take. I noticed that it wasn't just me who enjoyed my Dad's company either, lots of others seemed too as well. He was more of an outgoing person than Grandpa was around others off the farm, but he was godlike to me just the same.

Casting our lines into the glasslike surface of the pond I expected another opportunity to watch and learn. His cast was smooth, and I had mimicked the same motions, not quite making it as far as him. Now we waited, a test of our patience. This was it. Something he was showing me how to have.

As I sat on the bank my mind began to wander. I hated remembering that this wonderful time up in Iowa was only temporary. That this time with Dad would soon end and I'd be back to my permanent life with Bill. I drifted, wishing I lived here with my Dad but was snapped back quick believing that probably would never happen. My mom had something called "custody" of my sisters and me. Which, I assumed, meant she owns us. As I looked over to my Dad holding his pole, I think for a second of asking him "Why don't you have 'custody' of me? Why was it that Mom had to own me?" I wanted so badly to ask him, but the thought quickly passed, when I felt a nibble on my line. "Patience." I immediately thought of remembering what I was being taught. My Dad looked over and saw what had ensued and simply raised a hand up. Palm forward to signal 'wait'. That's all it took for me to follow his request. For me to listen to him he didn't need to say anything at all. He didn't need to yell. By raising a hand, he was easily saying to me, "Hold on Cody, let the fish bite the whole thing first. Don't get too excited," That is what I heard and what I did. I couldn't seem to push away the thought that it was not as it was with Bill knowing full well that this would have played out as a completely different event.

So, I sat on the bank with Dad waiting for the fish to grab hold of the whole thing, working overtime on my patience, hoping to show him I was capable. I hated having two Dads. Bill made me call him dad too, so in my head, I ran it as if I had two dads. Mom had left my 'real' Dad, the one sitting next to me on the riverbank, when I was younger. I was told it happened when I was four, but I don't remember. I'd never seen them talk, not once. They didn't even say anything to each other when they called to speak to us. Now that we had caller ID, we just answer ourselves, not involving them. We would pick up the phone when we saw the Iowa area code. They didn't even interact when they'd drop us off halfway for the weekends. We would just get out and slowly walk to the other car because we weren't sure what kind of emotions we were supposed to show. When we left Mom's car and walked the long-distance across the gas station parking lot into our Dad's car, we didn't run and skip, though we sure wanted to. But we didn't want Mom getting jealous or Bill getting angry. Even though we'd eek with excitement, we knew to wait until we got into Dad's car to show it. The same couldn't be said for the other way around when we got into Mom's car with Bill in it. We all dreaded it, but I was the one terrified of him. Even though it wouldn't take place until tomorrow, the thought of it gave me a sick feeling in my stomach. Just the thought of the 'drop-off' itself, the switching of us kids. I tried to shut it out, tried to focus on the fishing with my Dad but I was having a hard time at it. My Dad must have sensed something in me when he said, "What's wrong buddy?" That did bring me immediately back to the riverbank and I noticed I was tightly squeezing the fishing pole in my hand. As I eased off the handle of the rod my knuckles turned back to normal color, faded from white as blood returned to them. "Nothing," I lied. "Just daydreaming," I continued. I had lied and felt bad about it. I had noticed that when I started thinking about Bill I could sometimes get caught listening to this voice in my head. I didn't like it but wasn't exactly sure how to ignore it.

"I wonder why they don't talk?" I continued thinking as my Dad and I packed up and headed back to his house. We did catch a few nice fish after all. I knew that Dad and I would clean them when we got back, and he would probably give them to some of the elderly people in town. He often said, "They will enjoy eating our catch more than us." I did understand because he seemed to always be giving to others. This confused me because I couldn't make it work with his and mom's lack of interaction. "If they don't like each other why can't they just forgive each other?" I was thinking as I opened the truck door and climbed in. My dad fired it up and we headed back towards town. At Catholic school on Wednesday nights, I had learned about the word forgiveness. It seemed easy enough to do, as it was explained. That thing we learned God often does if someone simply asks for it. "Why didn't they ask each other for it?" I wondered as the truck bounced down the road. "I mean, they made my sister and I go to church and learn about this stuff so surely they must believe in it too," I remembered doing it myself a few weeks prior. I'd been forgiven and it was fairly easy. I had gone into that cramped little box in the back of the church and asked Father for some forgiveness. He said that was all I had to do. Just ask for it and God would do it, forgive me that is. That day I had told Father I was sorry for purposely pushing my sister off her bike. I truly meant to do it at the moment but later that night I cried about it too. Thinking back on how she had skinned her knee in the fall, I had this bad feeling of myself. Terrible, as a matter of fact. So, when Father told me I was 'forgiven' I felt a whole lot better. It seemed to help me.

The fish were now cleaned. It was a messy chore, but a necessary one. Dad had taught me not to waste anything and said often, "You or someone should always eat what you catch." He decided tonight it would be us and not the old men in town. I was happy. It had been an amazing day at Grandma's swimming and then fishing with Dad. He had gone to sleep early but my sisters and I were enjoying popcorn and a movie with our Stepmom. She didn't care if we called her Deb, so we did. It wasn't long before I noticed my eyes getting pretty heavy. Between the long day and the recently eaten dinner I was still awake enough to ask myself "I wonder how tomorrow will go during the drop-off?" This bounced in my head as the movie played in the background. My sisters were deeply lost in it.

Amber was ten, a year older than me and Leah was a year younger. Although they did a pretty good job of not letting anyone see that the relationship between our real mom and dad affected them, I knew it did. I felt as though I was their protector. Protector from Bill.

After failing the second-grade last year I finally made it to third. The teacher said I had a tough time spelling and math was an issue too. I would be lying to myself if I didn't admit that I also 'acted up' a lot. The teachers had their thoughts on why and I heard them say things like "Cody, is seeking attention." I saw it as I was just trying to find a way to 'fit in'.

"Ka-Boom!" A loud noise had jolted me awake. "I guess I was pretty tired. I must have been dreaming all that." I thought as I rubbed my eyes. Deb had noticed me bring my hands to my face. "Why don't you go lay down Cody," she insisted. I paused for a second before I responded, then I thought about the voice. I didn't want to hear the voice. All the things I had thought about during the day were still on my mind. And the voice. I knew it was pretty strong at night. I had these things they said were called 'Night Terrors." Sometimes I'd wake up screaming. It was the worst dream ever. Always the same. Something would be yelling at me and it wouldn't stop. A loud voice that seemed to want to hurt me. It was terrifying. I'd always wake up crying. Usually with soiled sheets too. That was the most embarrassing part. I still didn't dare go to sleepovers. "I'm good. I can stay awake," I lied. I wanted to delay the dreams for as long as possible. Tomorrow would come soon enough and all this fun would be over. I would try to make it last just a little bit longer as I refocused on the movie.

One year later, I grabbed my gear and walked off the Basketball court. For some reason my mind was wandering back to the 'hand off' between the parents in Iowa last summer. It had played out just like I'd predicted it would while fishing with my Dad a couple of days earlier. My sisters and I walked across the no man's land between the two cars parked in their neutral positions. Though we were sad to be leaving Dad's, we didn't show it. We put on our artificial smiles and climbed into the vehicle with my Mom and Bill. We had stepped into the pressure cooker. We genuinely loved our Mom. Just 'not so much' the counterpart sitting next to her. "What kind of mood was he in?" I knew it was important to ask myself as I climbed in the vehicle that day. "Which person was Bill today?" Which person was Bill this hour?" I had continued.

Now that the game was over, and I would be running into him shortly I began to ask myself the same questions about him. My guessing game had begun, and the answers would quickly reveal themselves. A Jekyll and Hyde character he was to me. Based on two things going on during the game I could usually pre-determine what kind of mood he would be in. By my performance and by the amount of yelling he did from the stands. I knew full well that I could control the latter by the kind of performance I'd have, so I played hard. I coupled that with the aggression I was able to harness, and I quickly found sports to be my outlet. My cure for a moment in time from Bill. I realized and loved the fact that the voice didn't talk when I was playing sports either. I must have been too busy focusing on winning. Besides, I was motivated to excel as I found I was getting positive encouragement from my coaches. Men that were building me up. Something I wasn't used to getting when I was with Bill.

As I climbed into the vehicle after what I knew had been a pathetic performance, I predicted Bill would be in a poor mood. I braced myself. As the barrage of questions came, I simply tried to 'tune out' his yelling. But the repeated "Why didn't you?" and the heated "You should have!" this and that's were all pushing against me. As his aggression was rising, the voice now speaking in my head was getting louder too. I knew this would soon climax probably ending with me getting swatted, but I seemed powerless to stop it. Seeing the spittle flying from his mouth, it didn't appear to me as though he was even paying attention to the road. I finally spoke, "I did my best! Please, can you pay attention to the road, you're scaring me," the words flew from my mouth. I knew immediately it was not the response he wanted to hear. He jerked the vehicle to the shoulder of the road and flung it into park. "This isn't going to be good," I told myself as he got out. Then I heard another voice, the one that always increased during these fight or flight moments. The voice that gave me courage. The voice that told me to do things I otherwise wouldn't do. "Hit him back!" I heard it say.

...WITH-IN THE COACHES

It was amazing what I could do with sports. As I got better and better, sports became a place of peace for me. I gained respect from other players and coaches alike, and the attention felt good. I played almost every sport. Getting that attention from other kids, kept me out of the house for hours. A triple win for me. I played almost every sport. Hockey, soccer, basketball, and football. It became something I just couldn't stop thinking about and the coaches loved me for it too. These men were the ones that would instill bravery into me. I was scared to even tackle someone when I first stepped onto the football field. I was afraid of getting hurt. "Just have a little Faith and Courage" my coach would tell me. If my coaches would have told me to jump off a bridge, I was certain I'd do it. I didn't seem to have a problem with trust in them. "Is that what Faith is?" I began asking myself. My Grandma had used the word before and I had heard it in Church, "But what is faith?" I continued wondering. The coaches were men of Honor to me, godlike humans. They yelled like Bill did but I sensed it was different, more purposeful in the sense. The purpose was not to break me down. So, I worked hard to show the coaches that I would be the last kid to ever break down. I started on every squad, in every sport. Coaches wanted me out there, in the game. I was always a starter. "Get Cody the ball!" I'd hear them shouting. It felt good to gain their attention. It felt good to have them need something from me. Quite possibly it was a hole in my life, that for a moment in time, was being filled. The hole when my real Dad wasn't there with me. Coaches became my fill-in Dad. It seemed the deeper bonds I wanted to have with my Dad weren't being built up enough with just the few weekends I would spend with him. The coaches in my life seemed to me to be filling the gap. The gratification I craved was being received through every sports season. I didn't take a single youth sports season off. The harder I worked the more they cheered me on too. The more I was cheered on, the better I felt.

Another year later, with another practice over and another tense car ride nearly done, I was about to find out when I got home this time, what kind of mood of the day Bill was in. I was walking on eggshells around this stepdad of mine lately. We'd begun arguing about some meaningless chore that in his eyes hadn't been done perfectly by me. It seemed to be a catalyst to a fight that Bill was looking for.

But it seemed more than that as if he needed some release himself from a bad day at work or maybe he was thinking it was a bad decision getting married to a woman with three kids. I wasn't sure which it was or if it was either, but I was getting more and more annoyed that he seemed gunning once again for me to get his release. "Let him get upset. Better yet, let him come at me." I was thinking as the car parked and our makeshift family piled out. As my hand reached for the knob of the front door I stopped in my tracks when I heard his shout of my name. "Cody, get the basketball! First one to twelve.". My pent-up emotions immediately began flowing through me. I was about to release aggression that I had let slowly pressurize for just these types of moments. For these times when Bill wanted to play me in a one on one game. My mind began speaking to me, "Win or lose he'd better believe I'm going to lay it all out there. The coaches called it 'giving 100%', well, I'm going to give it 120%!" I was ready to meet him once again on the makeshift home basketball court. The one Bill had erected for my Birthday. But to me, it was his, not mine. I had wanted nothing to do with it. I had asked for something different for my birthday, but I got the hoop regardless of my request.

I wasn't trying to impress Bill whenever I met him on the court. I didn't seem to care about his approval. What I wanted more than anything was to beat him in front of my mother. I wanted her to recognize I was good enough to beat him. With Bill, an athlete himself, these games between us had evolved into a nightly 'who could beat who in what?' Eventually, I had discovered that lifting weights on the small set of Bills in the basement was not only making me stronger but was becoming a better athlete. "Perfect!" I thought one day while lifting. "I'll become the biggest, badass athlete on the planet.".. It seemed as if I was willing to dedicate my entire existence to beat Bill. The weights were helping me speed this process up. "I just want to go to bed one night victorious." I would say to drive myself on. I did this to earn Bill's respect, not his approval. Not in a fatherly way either. It was for me more in a 'rival athlete' way. And just maybe if I beat him, he would start treating me like a man and stop yelling at me.

I soon recognized that sports seemed to stop the fighting at home too. Sports helped me gain recognition from my coaches. Sports kept me out of the house when I wanted to be. Sports released aggression from the frustrations I had when I missed my dad. I hoped that sports were going to get Bill to tell my mom that I was better than him. Sports became my life. I never thought about what I'd ever do without sports. I couldn't imagine it ever ending. My mind continued to say "Other kids would get hurt sometimes but not me. I'll never get hurt. I am going to try my hardest to be what I want to be." From deep-down I heard myself say, "I want to be a college athlete. One of those guys everybody looks up to. One of the best. No, I want to be the best!"

...WITH-IN MYSELF!

I racked the weight and sat up from the bench, breathing heavily after the set. Many more challenging drop-offs had occurred and a lot more fights with Bill had too. I wasn't sure what I was becoming or what Bill had created in me, but I knew one thing; I was unstoppable when it came to sports. It all started with using Bill's plastic weight set in the basement. That catapulted my performance in the sports arenas. Yet, I didn't care about that as much as I cared about something that was becoming evident, I could almost take him. I fell in love with getting bigger and stronger in order to do that. In the 1 on 1 games we played outback or the wrestling matches that ensued, I was getting closer and closer to victory over him each time. I still walked on eggshells around Bill, but as I grew stronger I became less and less afraid. The tension in him that always seemed to arise from a bad day at work or a bad decision, I just expected now. The temper was always right there with it, but I didn't try to rationalize it anymore. It was just part of who he was.

I was building myself into a person who could cope with it, who could handle it. I began to feel as though physical strength could solve all my challenges, having two that mattered most: Being the best at sports and showing Bill I wasn't afraid of him. Thinking on it I recognized I had one more challenge that was quite problem too, but I felt maybe I knew that I would never be able to solve it. It was actually a big one, in fact the biggest one: Never being able to get my Mom and Dad to be civil with one another, to forgive each other. It seemed beyond my power. They still hadn't talked, and it ate at me inside when I tried to understand it. This God, this person everyone, including my parents was making me learn about, He forgave. The one thing I knew, the one thing that had me sitting on the edge of my seat in Bible School and Church was when they would talk about that thing called forgiveness. "You should never hold hatred in your heart, it creates emptiness," I had heard Father say one day. "Emptiness. Hatred," I thought. "That's what I feel about Bill. I wonder if I could ever forgive him?" I asked. To me, it seemed as though getting bigger would be much more doable, much more realistic. "I don't need forgiveness, I need to get stronger," I started telling myself. With the help of a voice, I began to formulate my first opinion against God. Against the 'Word' I was being taught. If my parents had found an alternative to forgiveness, so could I. "Why forgive when you can forget? Why forgive when there are so many more alternatives?" I surmised. Divorce seemed to be a decent enough alternative to forgiveness, lots of parents did it? So, could this body I was building be a substitute for forgiveness. It could be my alternative to forgiving Bill. Then, I wouldn't need to forgive Bill, I would just need to be bigger than him. Stronger than him. As I laid down on the bench for another set, I was congratulated by the voice for my brilliant deductions. I was assured by that voice in my head that I had made a grand plan indeed. Little did I know the emptiness would grow with it. Little did I know the void, the gap would soon widen.

I pushed out one more rep in the basement than the last complete set and sat up. "Cody, get up here," Bill yelled. I got up from the bench and began climbing the stairs with a smile on my face. I didn't know what he wanted, and I didn't care. I also didn't realize that as I climbed the stairs my fists were beginning to clench tight, and the color of my knuckles was fading to whiter and whiter. Not clenched and fading by grabbing the bar for another lift of weights, but in preparation for the possibility of another kind of lift.

...WITH-IN THE WEIGHTS

As the years passed, nearing the end of Junior High, I didn't need Bill's weight set anymore. I began to excel in sports and had gained enough notoriety and with it, new benefits. This soon allowed me to hitch 4:30 a.m. rides with some of the coaches to lift weights at the gym. We'd push each other when there, lifting real weights not the plastic ones like I'd used over the previous year. I quickly fell in love with it. I loved pushing Coach Davis and Coach Willis, and they seemed to love pushing me. We'd all achieve personal records every week, patting each other on the back after a set of bench presses or squats. Affirmation from my mentors seemed everything I wanted and needed. The weights to build muscle, the attention to fill the void from my Dad not being nearby. This became everything to me. Lifting weights and playing sports became my outlet for so many things, I couldn't imagine life without it. I didn't want to think of it. Life without sports was something that I never thought possible. Sports gave me another benefit, in fact, the biggest one. The longer I was in the gym or at practice, the longer I was away from Bill. Away from the chaos at home.

It became somewhat of an obsession to me. I relished in the fact that I was growing into something everyone recognized. Before school, I started running with the cross-country team. This along with lifting with the coaches. After school, I would go to 3-hour practices that would end at 6 pm. When most kids went home to eat dinner with their families, I did not. Instead, not having a car yet, I'd run the 3 miles from the school to the local community center to lift weights for another 2 hours. I knew I wasn't old enough to use the gym, but nobody ever said anything to me, so I lifted anyway. I would push myself harder and longer than any of the other kids and it began to show. I was even starting to get bigger than some of the coaches. The recognition was at hand. Still, I felt I needed more. I felt I needed to be as big and strong as the biggest guys in the gym, like the guys in the magazines. I also felt I needed to be captain of the football team, become an all-state athlete, and go play college football, something only the best kids ever got to do. I wanted it all. The bar was continually rising, and I'd be dammed if I'd fail to meet it. To let my coaches down on the field, the same coaches that I lifted with would mean I had failed. I would never be average; I would never let them down.

I would soon find out that the community center near my house was home to a large bodybuilding competition. One evening after lifting I snuck into the auditorium side door and gawked at the large, muscled bodies flexing on stage. The people clapping, the oohs, the awes, and the attention. "I wonder how long it will take for me to get that big," I tried to guess. "Is there any techniques, tricks, or tools I can use to speed up this process, anything at all?" I continued asking myself as I looked down at my deflated arms, seen now in comparison to the ones on stage? I went home that evening and Googled a simple question, "How to get big fast?" The top results kept talking about these things called 'anabolic steroids'. "Whatever are they anyway? " I began asking myself. Then again, "Do I really care what they are?" came the rapid reply. "If they will make me bigger and stronger and faster, I wanted them and I wanted them now." a convincing voice now speaking into this phase of my life. One that did not care to speak about the finer details of such things. Listening to this voice seemed to be working out just fine for me. So, past the momentary caring came "I need anabolic steroids."

As I lay in bed that evening tired from another lift, I pondered some previous thoughts. "Other kids get hurt sometimes but not me; I'll never get hurt. I'll always be on the field, on the courts, lifting weights, getting better, and getting bigger. Nothing can stop me." The last thing came before sleep, "How do I go about getting those steroids? I guess tomorrow I'll just have to Google that."

9

THE DEEPER DARKER
STATE OF MIND...

...LESSNESS

Driving in his car Cody found himself asking God for forgiveness. His sin, now much more significant than when he was the boy asking the Priest to forgive him for pushing his little sister off her bike. He was in much deeper than in those days. His place of confession, no longer a booth in the back of the Church. It was now a car, his car. He asked God directly "Forgive me for the overdose, the drug dealing, the womanizing, and everything else that has come of my life?" Cody felt he was living nothing but the life of a 'Thug'. Not a brother or a son, but a 'Thug'. Since the time college ended and he had moved to Omaha, he felt a growing emptiness inside. A space that needed filling, though he struggled to define what was creating the space itself. Yet, he knew it had created an uncomfortable pain. He may not have known from where it came but he did know the one thing that took it away, Fentanyl. He also knew an undefinable piece of Himself had gone missing. He knew that he was filling that missing piece with all those things he now prayed to God for the forgiveness of. He was praying that God would help him find a way out. He felt the life he was living couldn't last much longer, and knew it had a life expectancy of its own making, with but two options, Death or Prison. He began to accept those things. Then, embrace them. He began listening to artists who spoke of this life as well, fellow 'Thugs'. Cody found that he felt better when listening to someone he could relate to. Still driving he grabbed his phone, lost in the Hodge Podge talk with God he clicked on the song "Hail Mary" by Tupac. His favorite rapper. His favorite song. When he first heard the 90s rap song back in High School, he liked it but didn't enjoy it as much as he did now, playing it all the time. He felt the lyrics helped him accept who he was. Whenever he felt nervous, he'd click it on. Lots of things could spark its call. In this instance, it was the cop car that had pulled up next to him. He clicked 'play' and Tupac's voice began blaring through his speakers. The cop and Cody made eye contact. Cody smiled.

"Come with me
Hail Mary
Run, Quick see
What do we have here now?
Do you want to Ride or Die?
La, da, da, da, da, da"

"This is Tupac's attempt at prayer through a song," Cody thought. Mumbling the lyrics to the song and still attempting his own. Two men, Tupac and Cody, seemingly lost beyond repair. Both fully aware. Knowing in their hearts, as the words from the chorus laid out. "Ride or Die". A famous phrase used by well-known men who come to certain roadblocks in life. "Continue down the path I'm on and eke out survival, or don't," Cody thought. He smiled and, at that moment, he thought about getting the phrase tattooed on his other side. "If I was going to die. At least everyone would know

I'd accepted it by the Ride or Die on my side." Cody thought. "It's too bad Tupac got the latter. Twenty-something years old with his entire life ahead of him," Cody thought while shaking his head. He had been too young to remember when the California rapper got shot and killed. Cody was beginning to feel that his 29-year-old self probably didn't have much longer at this thing called 'life' either. He could feel it in his health. He could see it in his tired face, every time he looked in the mirror. The Fentanyl and steroids had been taking their toll on him. He felt more like 40. Dying from drug issues wasn't Cody's immediate concern though. It was if given the choice, which one would he pick, Death or Prison? He tried to resume praying to God, hoping that He was listening.

Cody smiled at the cop next to him at the red light, but he felt uneasy. The light turned green, and their eyes looked forward, breaking the stare at one another. As Tupac's voice continued echoing through the car speakers Cody spoke out loud "I'm not the only one that hopes. I suppose that's why they say you got to have Faith." With the lyrics blasting through the speakers, he was now using Tupac's prayer as his own. "Are you listening?" he asked God. "What if my faith isn't strong enough?" now talking into his windshield. His hand's gripped tighter on the leather steering wheel. The steering wheel he used to navigate night after night, on his steroid drops. The leather made a popping noise as his fist tightened. The lyrics, clearly moving him. He felt a hot flash physically circulating through him. He wasn't sure if it was from the music or the lack of Fentanyl in his system. He needed a shot. The voice in his head, not yet louder than Tupac's. "Are you listening?" Cody yelled in his car yet inaudible to anyone even with the windows down. Still searching for an answer back. He wanted an answer from God, and he wanted it right then.

"Let's go deep into the solitary mind
of a madman who screams
In the dark, evil lurks
Enemies see me flee
Activate my hate, let it break
To the Flame"

Cody pictured himself sitting in a cell-like the man in Tupac's prayer. Alone. Truly, alone. He wondered what it would feel like in solitary confinement. Wondered if he'd be strong enough to make it or eventually crack and "Scream in the dark" as the lyrics said. Cody then thought about the last three words in the verse "To the Flame". Still moved, still upset, he was driving but he wasn't focused on the road. That feeling when you arrived somewhere in your car and wonder how you got there. Lost in thought the entire time. Daydreaming. Cody felt in that moment the same thing had happened with his life. Sleepwalking through a mess he couldn't explain. He hadn't blinked since putting the song on, or so it felt. "To the Flame." Cody thought again. For the first time in his life, he wondered if he would go to Hell instead of Heaven. The flame in Cody's life was nipping at his heels. He felt it. The skulls on his body, proof the adversary was close. He rubbed his chest; he could feel something closing in.

"Institutionalized I live my life,
a product made to crumble
But to hardened for a smile,
too crazy to be humble
We Ballin'

Catch me, Father, please cause I'm fallin'.
In the liquor store, pass the Hennessy I hear it callin',
Hail til I reach Hell
I ain't scared

"An Oxymoron if there ever was one," Cody thought. "Hail till I reach Hell." The lyrics still reverberating through his head. The oxymoron he was living. Praying to God with drugs in his car, drugs soon to be in his system. Him and Tupac, just being honest to God, he chooses to suppose. Cody knew he was but one of the thousands of young men that cranked the song and thought it was meant for them. He knew he was no different from millions of Christians all over America. Hailing God till they reach Hell. Cody wouldn't be surprised how he got there though. He smiled, thinking about the present-day 'Christian'. They all pray as good Christians do. An outward fraud that eventually holds no water with God. "He knows what you're doing, he knows the truth," Cody thought. "At least I can accept myself and meet the Devil not questioning how I got there" he continued. The words of the lyrics doing what they always did for him. Giving him the acceptance of the life, he was living. "At least Tupac's keeping it real," Cody thought. "I can respect that. Someone who can admit their faults. Not hide behind a white picket fence and a bible" now slightly gritting his teeth. "I'd follow a man like that. Despite his flaws. Why can't people like Tupac lead a congregation?" not able to stop the thoughts? Passing a church in his car and shaking his head at the people milling around the parking lot. He slowed down and turned the volume up. "They pray for me, ha-ha, I pray for them. Fake, all fake." thinking as he passed the church.

"I got ahead with no screws in it
What can I do?
One life to live but I got nothing to lose
Just me and you.
On a one-way trip to prison
We all wrapped up in this life we're living
Life as thugs"

"Life as thugs." Cody laughed at the last verse that blast out his open window, actually hoping the churchgoers heard it. "You probably think 'Thugs' are young black kids walking the streets. Thugs are you." Cody said. Pointing at the parking lot passing by. "Probably more thugs right there than in the inner cities." he continued, pointing a thumb behind him over his shoulder, "They love to do the easy shit and pray. How many of you so-called Christians are walking the walk too? Putting in the work to help humanity?" Cody wondered. Tupac still blaring in the background. Cody grabbed his phone. Decided he had to hear the last verse again. He was so pissed about his previous thoughts passing the church that he decided to rewind the music and get back into the zone.

"I got ahead with no screws in it
What can I do?
One life to live but I got nothing to lose
Just me and you.
On a one-way trip to prison
We all wrapped up in this life we're living
Life as thugs"

"Just me and you, on a one-way trip to prison." The lyrics resonating with Cody. "You'll come with me, won't you?" Cody questioning God. "You coming with me when this all comes crashing down?" he continued. No answer. As always, no answer.

"To my homeboys in Quentin Max, doing they bid
raise hell to this real shit
and feel this.
When they turn out the lights,
I'll be there in the dark
Thug'n eternal through my heart
Now Hail Mary"

"Thug'n eternal through my heart," Cody thought. Respecting Tupac's drive, his commitment to the game. The life of the streets. Tupac made it pretty clear he wouldn't stop. Death and prison didn't scare Tupac and Cody wanted to believe they didn't scare him either. Tupac spoke to a generation of incarcerated men. Cody questioned if they had what it took, the mindset Tupac rapped about. Right then he felt something rise in him. That old familiar feeling his inability to quit something he'd started. The one thing that started so young with Bill and ended with the day he stepped off the field with the ESPN cameras rolling. The National Championship games. His fourth and final one. He had loved being part of that brotherhood. Found himself in those teams. "Thug'n eternal through my heart." Cody wanted to 'quit' this life though he wondered at the same time if it was eternal in his heart.

"When they turn out the lights,
I'll be there in the dark
Thug'n eternal through my heart
Now Hail Mary"

Tupac laid out those last four lines again. A repeat from the previous verse. Words Cody wanted to resonate with before another rapper jumped on the track and took over. "When they turn out the lights, I'll be there in the dark." A scene envisioned while he drove. Sitting in a dark prison cell. "Or was he talking about dying and being in the dark of Hell?" questioning what Tupac meant. Letting 'Thugs' around the world know he didn't care. "This seems to be a tough-ness few humans could probably endure. A prison sentence." Cody thought and decided two things. One, God was indeed talking back through his speakers, sending him signs he should bail, 'quit' everything. This wasn't football or another sport. It was something he could quit. He could quit. "In this case, it's ok to quit Cody," he told himself as if to permit himself the thought. "Move out of Omaha and never look back." he continued. "Tell your family you need help. Beat the voice in your head not by injecting more Fentanyl but by actually telling someone." He paused for a moment then picked the phone up. Scrolled through his contacts and got to the name he needed.

The name he wanted more than anything. Ready to end it all. For a minute, he was excited at the idea of quitting. He then did the second thing he decided. He clicked 'call' and the phone began ringing.

Juan picked up on the other end. "Hey man, I need another tattoo. It just came to me. I want "Thug Life" on my other side." Juan laughed, excited to see Cody come up on his text again and get back to work. They set up a time to meet the next day. Cody now with the decision made, couldn't wait. Of course, he'd need some Fentanyl to get through it. He wasn't going to bear this one out like last time, no matter how much Jesus looked upon him from the picture above. Cody started it over again.

"Come with me
Hail Mary…"

…GAMES

Cody had pledged to get the tattoo. To himself that is. An internal commitment. One put to action through a simple text message. The appointment was set with Juan, more serious yet. One step closer to getting the real deal. A non-formal form of committal in today's world, a text message. Semi-serious at best. Something Cody felt he could have backed out of but wouldn't.

Now, laying in a tattoo chair high on a cocktail of opiates with a needle pounding in and out of his skin, more serious yet. Backing out at this point wasn't an option. Well, unless Cody wanted a half-done tattoo on his body. Like many things up to this point in Cody's life, his commitment wasn't something to be played with. He was certain he wasn't going to tough this tattoo out like he had the last, the girl on his side. Matter of fact, he was higher than a kite and felt amazing.

One of the many ultimate installations of trust. A co-sign. A marriage. A tattoo. Cody and Juan's partnership were only skin deep, but they would always remember each other. "My first 'Thug Life' tattoo," Juan said. "I always wondered when I'd eventually do this one" he continued. The phrase. The Rapper. Most knew of Tupac's 'Thug Life' tattoo. At least that's what Cody thought as he laid there getting one of his own on his side. Justifying his decision. It wasn't a sun or some lame Chinese symbols. Some skulls or brass knuckles. It was a 'Thug Life' tattoo! "Much harder to explain if it ever needed to be. "I hope telling people the inspiration behind the tattoo doesn't involve relating a song to my downward spiraling life," Cody thought. "Death and Prison," he was thinking with one earbud in playing "Hail Mary". He sensed he would need Tupac's voice along with the Fentanyl in his system to get through this tattoo. The song, continuing to do what it did best for Cody; drowning the voice in his head and giving acceptance to the thought of the two roads he was surely heading towards. These two things he wondered how he got to the point of justifying, as somehow ok. He wasn't a boy learning how to swim with his Grandma. This was a risk much greater than had been expected. Juan hunched over Cody deep in concentration. The Jesus picture, now behind him. Cody was glad he couldn't see it.

Some onlookers, Juan's friends, stopped by his chair. They gawked at the tattoo being placed on Cody's skin, seeing bravery in placing something so ridiculous on his body. "You're one courageous soul for getting that tattoo," an onlooker said. Cody just nodded not wanting to get into a deep dialog about the tattoos meaning to him. His mind wandered about times courage had played a part in his life. "If she only knew," Cody thought while continuing to internalize the acceptance of those two ludicrous fates.

Cody wasn't sure if it was courage or stupidity. "Probably both," he thought. He hoped the next major act of courage would be quitting Fentanyl. "That'll be the day" as if an impossibility or maybe needless foolish thinking. With onlookers still standing over him mesmerized with Juan tattooing him. Cody glanced at his left tricep, 'Courage'. At his next session with Juan, he would get it covered up. He was tired of delaying it. Tired of hearing the words in his head.

"Doesn't that hurt? You seem to be handling that tattoo pretty well," another onlooker said. Cody smiled, a million things running through his head. "Hurt?" he thought. A word that's relatively benign to a Fentanyl addict. "A little," Cody responded, "but not much," "You do know what "Thug" is an acronym for, right?" the onlooker continuing to ask him questions. Cody wishing they'd leave. He wanted to be left alone. His tattoo therapy had turned into a show and tell. "No idea," Cody mumbled. Hoping they'd catch the clue in his voice and move on. "The Hate U Give," the onlooker said. Cody processing the words, didn't fully understand what he'd just heard. "The Hate U Give." Emotions began rising in him that he couldn't process. The Fentanyl was still doing its job. Immediately his thoughts gravitating towards his previous thought of "Death and Prison." If there was ever a thing that could cause more hate than those two things, Cody couldn't think of them. "The Hate U Give" Cody thought again. The skulls, the girl on his side. His use. His selling. His crumbling life. "The Hate U Give". His thoughts, his actions. Everything in his life, proof of 'it' taking control of him. 'It' hating him, and him hating 'it' back. Cody hated himself at that very moment. Another tattoo, proof 'it' was indeed winning. Proof 'she' was indeed winning. "The hate 'she' gives," Cody thought. Cody knew at that familiar moment what 'she' was.

He was able to positively identify 'it'. The 'thing' he'd met twice before when overdosing. The 'thing' that had ensnared him and continued living inside him. 'It', 'she', the 'thing' was an addiction. They had a love/hate relationship with Cody, and he with them. A Thug Life of their own.

Finally, the onlookers moved on. Cody believed in miracles but couldn't put a finger on whether or not he'd just been part of one. Signs from God. "What would it eventually take to beat my addiction? Without death or prison?" Cody thought, then of the picture behind him. He laughed when the answer abruptly came to him and he responded "Your right. I suppose it would take an act of God." Tupac was still playing in his ear, rapping about his acceptance of the ideals. His life had ended that way. Cody was now hoping he wouldn't. But, without an 'act of God' Cody was also certain his course had been set. And if he could somehow dodge death. That would still leave him with one more option.

With the 'Thug Life' tattoo now healed; Cody waited for his friend. Another Fentanyl user he trusted. The only one he trusted. He needed to drop off the money for his portion and discuss the deal.

Meanwhile, Cody's 'trusted' friend got the appropriate recording equipment set up by the DEA agents.

Cody continued waiting and looking out his front door for his friend to pull up. A few black SUVs had circled his house. "The neighbors must have bought new vehicles." Cody convinced himself. His smart TV played a song from his phone.

A Tupac song.

10

THE CARDS TUMBLE...

...WITH RELEASE

Cody was walking on a treadmill warming up before starting his 'Senior Circuit' class. After Jason had opened a couple of new fitness gyms in Omaha, they decided it would be pretty cool to bring a new program for the seniors to the gym. Cody gained plenty of experience with that demographic, older people, from his internship at Northwest. He worked out there in the mornings anyway so, "Why not run a class before I work out?" Cody thought. It made perfect sense, so that's what Cody did. Getting back to training like he had when he first came to Omaha. Only now, it was Jason's gym, and he wasn't pressured for sales and commissions. He came to the gym, ran his class and that was it. Plus, Cody found enjoyment in helping the older population get back into shape. It was a win-win for everyone. It was here, in Jason's gym, while Cody was waiting for his class to start that the Feds decided to bust him.

Cody thought he had seen an abnormal amount of police cruisers that morning when he drove in. He had grown somewhat comfortable in ignoring or attempting to ignore this type of activity anyway so as not to become paranoid. His chosen profession required such conditioning for mental survival. Even seeing a couple now parked across the street at the gas station as he pulled open the doors to Jason's gym early that morning, he said to himself "No big deal. They're probably just getting coffee and donuts." The two black SUVs that pulled up in the parking lot in front of him while he walked on the treadmill reminded him immediately of the ones he'd seen in front of his house the day he waited for his friend to consummate 'The Deal'. "Nothing out of the ordinary," he worked to convince himself. The vehicles to Cody seemed an ominous representation of his soon-to-crumble life. As if red flags pointing to a massive event that was too late to prevent, even if he didn't pay them any mind. He could ignore it all if he wanted to. Or he could put on another Tupac song and pretend it would all be ok. But somehow, he knew in his heart right then and there, it was all about to end.

They were soon to be among him. Though he continued to walk on the treadmill he knew exactly what was happening. Cody then did two things together that even he wouldn't have predicted himself to do in such an open environment. He smiled, then cried.

They now reeked of cops and looked like cops in every sense of the word, yet Cody continued walking on the treadmill. A peacefulness engulfing him, within his tears. He wasn't high, but at that moment, as he saw his new life unfolding, he felt higher than any drug he had ever taken. At that moment he came face to face with the power Fentanyl had over him and knew the relationship with her was about to end. As the cops opened the front door, he saw a glimpse of 'her', his addiction. She was hideous. Something was happening that she never wanted to have happen, for her road through his life to end, or for there to even be a possibility of an end. Cody really felt that. Heard it in her voice still attempting to work on him.

He wanted a shot of Fentanyl more than anything but knew he wouldn't get one. The wolf in sheep's clothing, about to be exposed. "These cops know what I've been up to," Cody's thoughts seemed sure, "they are going to arrest me and lock me up. What will I do without Fentanyl?" He knew his thoughts were beginning to race as he was foreseeing a very real problem before his eyes. The realization was unattractive, to say the least.

Cody's buried addiction. It was all about to be brought into the light, and she knew it. It was horrifying at first. A pain that couldn't be readily subdued. All these emotions came crashing down like a wave on Cody's head. No shot of drugs to bury it. And all the while she stood there in her nakedness, ugly. The thing that had been trying to kill him, his addiction.

"Mr. Lanus we are with the Nebraska State Patrol and Drug Enforcement Agency. Can you come with us please?" He took a deep breath and stepped off the treadmill and followed the two agents outside. Cody knew it was serious, they weren't cops, identifying themselves only as "agents", something much more series to a layman. "We have a search warrant for your house and phone" they continued. Cody, red-eyed and now with a half-cocked grin on his face pulled his phone from his pocket and held it in the air. One of them snatched it from His hands. He didn't care saying, "Take it." Cody didn't care about the damn phone. All he wanted to do was say one thing and when he spoke it out, they froze as if not able to comprehend what they'd just heard. Cody had said, "Thank you."

...WITH RELIEF

They didn't cuff him. They didn't need to. To him, he'd been res-cued. Something he saw no need in fleeing from. He didn't need to guess anymore. Death or Prison? He knew which one he'd reached. A Tupac song he'd willed into existence. 'His' existence. For him, you could have put the Federal Agents up there with the Narcan that had previously brought him back to life, Guardian Angels. He didn't want to hurt them he wanted to hug them.

He told the manager at the gym he'd have to cancel the class for the day, "something big came up," he told him. "Life-changing as a matter of fact," he continued. He'd probably be gone for longer than a day but "Nobody needed to know that" Cody thought as he walked out the front door of the gym with Federal Agents in front and behind him. Cody climbed into the front seat of a black SUV and began the trek back home to the other side of Omaha with the DEA. The convoy he was part of, the vehicles that had swarmed the gym. He felt famous in a sense. The last time he had police escorts was the National Championship game he played in during college. The very last football game he'd played in. "I wonder what my coaches would think now," he thought.

Breaking the silence an agent in the back seat spoke up, "Your pack-age has been intercepted."

He deduced immediately it was the order he had placed a few days prior. He knew in his gut what had happened. He didn't want to accept it but definitely, he knew. He was certain who it was that had helped the Feds. These were the same black SUVs he had seen a few days earlier roaming around his house. As much as he wanted to ignore the truth he couldn't. He knew his friend had set him up.

"You're facing 20 years in Federal Prison for conspiracy to distribute Fentanyl. We expect total honesty from this point forward," the agent continued. The rest of the way to Cody's house they rode in silence. "20 years!" Cody thought sitting in the front seat of the SUV.

The convoy pulled up to Cody's house and was met by a barrage of other vehicles. "Between five and ten" Cody deduced. Men in bulletproof vests with 'DEA' and 'Federal Agent' written in yellow letters on the back of the vests stepped rapidly from all of them. They ran towards Cody's house, rifles in hand. Eyeball to scope. Doing the crouched running that is so often associated with soldiers. They surrounded Cody's house, pointing the guns at windows and doors. They stayed ready, waiting for some sort of signal as if from a man of higher rank. A man with a battering ram approached the front door. Ready to blast it off its hinges. An expense Cody deemed silently, "Ridiculous!". Doing what he thought sensible at that very moment, Cody reached into his pocket and fished for his keys. Within a microsecond, he was stopped by the sound of a hammer being cocked behind him. Cody froze, knew what the sound meant. "They're keys to the front door," Cody said. "Pull them out slowly," the agent replied. Cody did as he was told. Slowly holding the keys at shoulder length and jingling them. "You can just unlock the door. Nobodies inside. No need to mess my door up," Cody continued.

They took the keys from Cody and stormed in like Navy Seals as he watched from the black SUV, the agent still behind him. All Cody could think about as they raided his house was getting a fix, a shot. He wasn't thinking about the agents inside or the one sitting behind him with the gun. All he could think about was getting high. Anything would suffice: Fentanyl, Percocet, OxyContin, Vicodin- even Hydrocodone would do the trick. He'd take whatever he could get. The first bead of the sweat of withdrawal moved its way down Cody's face. He was sure that the Fed's intervention wouldn't in- volve a tapering off of opiates. "This won't be comfortable," Cody thought. Her grip, strong. Her roots, deep. Addiction.

A man in fatigues appeared at the front door. "Probably some sort of ex-military," Cody thought. He waved Cody and the agent behind him to get inside the house. This time Cody wouldn't make any sudden movements. He let the agent open his door.

Now inside Cody sat at his kitchen table with multiple Federal Agents asking a barrage of questions. Simple questions at first like why and how he got involved with Fentanyl to more complicated ones involving Cody's importing methods. "Let's get something straight," the head agent in charge said, "Aside from finding Jimmy Hoffa in your basement you'll be free on pre-trial release," He then went into detail about this thing he kept referring to as 'pre-trial release'. It appeared as a surprise to Cody, with his clean criminal history, he would be free to continue his life prior to a trial. Aside from drug selling and use, if he were able to fulfill the requirements of the pre-trial release, he would remain free. Clean urine, Cody was informed, would also be one of these stipulations. Cody was glad he would remain free, but then again, he kind of wished he wouldn't. What was swirling in his head on this news was "Could I maintain?"

Cody knew he had to be at work at his law-abiding job in a few hours. He wanted them to finish their search and leave. They already had boxes full of steroids and steroid-making equipment. All the things Cody and Jason had initially invested in to get the business going. Now, all being carried out in boxes by the Feds. "We need to bring you down to headquarters and get you processed in." an agent informed him. "Great," Cody thought "Another trip across Omaha with the agent behind me!" So, back to the black SUV, they went.

The DEA headquarters was literally a block from Jason's. You could have practically thrown a stone out of Jason's front door and hit their building; it was that close. "How Ironic," Cody thought with all the times they were dealing right there.

Once inside headquarters, the Feds did their thing. Fingerprints and paperwork that now identified Cody as some sort of soon-to-be 'inmate' or 'felon' of some kind. Cody wasn't sure which, "Probably both." he guessed.

With that part over Cody was left in a tiny holding cell waiting for the next phase to begin. "Whatever that may be," Cody thought. A couple of detainees next to him in the cell were yelling something in Spanish. "They must be having as good of a day as me," Cody said to himself. Sitting there he couldn't help but have his mind think about the impact of all this on his work. "What are my bosses going to think if they find out?" he thought. "I'll need to take a week of vacation; these next few days will be rough." Knowing the pain of the withdraws he was about to endure. The ones that were nipping at him already as he sat in the cell inside the DEA headquarters.

Thirty minutes later the cell door opened. An agent with a camera in his hand stood in the doorway. "We need to get a picture of all your tattoos," he said. "Tattoos?" Cody thought while standing and smiling as he pulled the shirt over his head giving the agent the first glimpse of his tattoo-covered torso and sides. Cody stood still, waiting for the agent's instructions. "Got any on your back?" the agent asked. He didn't need to say anything, Cody just turned. The 'Tribal Sun' on his shoulder blade and the Chinese symbols on each arm were easily visible for the agent to photograph. Snap. Cody saw the flash on the wall in front of him. A non-verbal queue that the picture had been taken. As he turned back around the agent asked, "What do those symbols mean?" Not seeming to need any formal answer, as he didn't have pen or paper, Cody deduced he was asking out of his own curiosity. Being a question Cody was by now used to answering he responded, "Faith and Courage,". "Well you're going to need a whole lot of both of those in the upcoming months." the agent seemed to joke. Now bringing the camera up to his face again. A face that resembled most of the other agents. Square Jaw. Neat hair. Ex-military. A face Cody thought he had seen before at one of the gyms he frequented. A face he probably 'had' seen at that very gym. "A cop's face," Cody thought. The agent continued snapping close-up pictures of Cody's chest and torso, the skulls in their various forms. When the agent went to photograph Cody's side, he naturally picked his arms up, resting his hands on his head. The girl tattoo was first. The agent this time getting close like a professional photographer. Snap. Snap. Cody felt like a piece of artwork. The agent next moved to the other side, to the 'Thug-Life' tattoo. He stopped for a second then raised the camera to his face asking as if perplexed through a laugh, "Why the fuck would you ever put that on your body?" Snap. Snap. The flash once again bouncing off the small concrete walls in the tiny cell with its stainless-steel toilet.

Just then, Cody was beginning to feel dizzy. He wanted to get out of there. He was defeated. He was tired. He was soon to be indicted.

While still thinking about how he should respond to the agent's "Thug-Life" question he heard himself blurt out the only thing that seemed to come. "It's a long story."

...WITH PAIN!

"You're a loser and you've amounted to nothing. 20 years! Do you really think you'll amount to anything after 20 years? You couldn't accomplish it before going into prison what makes you think you won't come out the same? A loser." The voice in his head, the addiction, was talking fast. She had now morphed into a full-blown monster. That thing, that 'voice' Fentanyl had subdued. That thing, that 'voice' steroids hid. That 'voice', manifested from lies Cody let himself believe as if true. She was born out of those lies. She thrived and grew from them. Now she was a gargantuan beast in full force exposing thoughts he wanted to keep buried. They were the storms that collided to create her, the addiction. The relationship he longed to have with his distant parents, the abrupt stop in athletics, and the way he saw himself in the mirror. All these were voids he'd created or at least had allowed to be created. All these lies he told himself. The voice inside him, now amplified by the physical withdrawal from the fentanyl, Cody was in bad shape. He felt broken.

Now home from the DEA headquarters and in this shape, Cody knew he couldn't go into work at Boys Town. "Not a chance," he thought. Grabbing his phone to call in 'sick', he knew he was indeed 'sick', drug sick. He called his boss. "I need a couple of days off. I've been hit with the flu," he lied. "Well, kind of," he convinced himself. The voice, the thing because of Fentanyl he hadn't had to deal with for a long time was now screaming for attention. Cody was sweating and shaking from the lack of opiates in his system. It felt like someone was pulling the atoms from his body and submerging them in ice water. He shivered. Then, when they started to freeze, just before they did, they were thrown into a furnace and set aflame. He poured out a cold sweat, immediate extremes of hot and cold. Cody wasn't sure which one he'd rather endure. But as he got up from the fetal position to shower, he knew it didn't matter. He would be left to endure both. Not the hot and cold but rather the 'voice' and the withdrawals.

After a long shower and a couple of shots of Vodka, Cody was able to wearily navigate through himself. The intense pain of the withdrawals and the voice now telling him to go ahead and end the agony before a federal judge got the chance. He began to believe her. Cody thought about the people he'd let down. His parents and ex-coaches he still communicated with. His friends and co-workers. "Take the easy way-out Cody," the voice's convincing words trying to work their way into reality. Somehow, he was able to push them away and navigate through it all. Now in his room, sitting on his bed, he stared at the vent covers the DEA had ripped off the walls and floor. His clothes had been thrown on the ground. His room was destroyed. He couldn't summon the energy to even imagine cleaning it. Then, Cody felt something different.

Sitting there, he felt a tug. Despite all the emotions being supercharged through his emotionally wrecked psyche, he felt a pull. What it was, he wasn't sure. But he thought it was coming from his nightstand where both drawers remained flung open, most of the contents still scattered on the floor.

He hadn't pulled the thing out for years. His prayers in his car had been sufficient enough. He looked to his left, down at the bottom drawer of his nightstand where he kept his Bible. "Yeah, that's definitely where it's coming from," Cody thought.

When he pulled the Bible from his nightstand it was dusty. It was the one Father Peter had given him a few years prior, or so he remembered. Then again, maybe it wasn't actually given to 'him', but the one he had accidentally, on purpose, walked out of work with. He remembered throwing it into his back seat that day. The Bible had actually made a few product drop-offs with him before finding a home in his nightstand. It's resting place for quite some time. In fact, it hadn't even been opened. As Cody sat there holding it, he noticed his thumbs had left prints on the smooth cover. The dust and oil from his skin coming together to form a visible print. The first ones of Cody's visible on a book of this nature and subject for quite some time.

Today he would become one of the Christians he had so often judged. The ones he saw that day in the parking lot while listening to Tupac. He would become another story of a broken human searching for answers. "An addict with a Bible." Cody laughed at himself attempting to find some resemblance of comfort within this reality. He opened the cover. It was new and stood erect on its own. Cody had to fold it down.

Like the Tupac song, "I wonder if I can relate to any of this stuff" Cody began wondering. He sat on his bed, Bible in both hands looking down and wondering "Where do I even begin?" He didn't know where to start, so, he started from the beginning. Sitting on his bed now facing a felony and drug sick from withdrawal Cody flipped the thin pages to the start. The pages, although weightless, felt as though pounds in his condition. He began to read, "In the beginning, God created the Heavens and the Earth. The Earth was without form and void, and darkness was on the face of the deep. And the spirit of God was hovering over the face of the waters."

While he was wondering if the God he was reading about was watching over the void and darkness that he convinced himself he was in, Cody mumbling the words "I wonder if God's going to help me get through this?" Just then, Cody noticed something. He wasn't feeling pain from the lack of opiates in his system anymore, but he was starting to feel better, feel ok. He was sure it wasn't the voice telling him lies this time. Instead in his rock bottom condition, he was sure he heard something different. In the depths that he lay, he was certain he heard it. He hadn't heard it like this before, hadn't cared to. Through all the praying he had done when he was younger and at Boys Town, he hadn't heard it like this. He'd only claimed he had before, but now he was certain he 'was'. Two words he heard, no more, no less. Despite what Cody heard, he was struggling to accept it as true.

Two words are all God said to him.

"I'm here."

11

'COUNTY' A TASTE OF FREEDOM

Standing in front of the mirror, I rubbed my chest. My fingers lightly gliding across the skulls on my skin. I looked down at my stomach. The mirror in my jail cell wasn't large enough to reflect them all. I looked at the unfinished skull with the gas mask and the unfinished brass knuckles. I thought of Kevin in that 'Horror Shop' of a tattoo parlor where much of what I was seeing began. I closed my eyes and shook my head as I recalled the events of the last year. It was painful but not like the kind of pain getting the tattoos had been. This was much different. A much more difficult pain. The pain of the sudden realization of my wreckage.

Thoughts that were hard to relive were roaming through my head, brought on by tattoos that were hard to see. I turned sideways and held my triceps up to the small mirror. Looking at the tattoos "Faith and Courage," thinking I was now glad I never had them covered. I'd gone down a much darker road since the more wholesome tattoos I had inked on me before entering college. During a time when I would never have believed, I'd end up in the place I was now standing. The graffiti etched mirror I looked into, was made of jailhouse glass, of course, plastic, but it did a decent enough of a job reflecting what I needed to see, myself.

I moved on to view the tattoos on my sides. I looked down on them, twisting from one side to the other and back again thinking over the reasons I got them. The last few years were a blur I wasn't sure how to process. "How could I have done all this, allowed all this, wanted all this?" I asked myself. "Am I really alive or is this some sort of purgatory I'm living in?" I continued. Momentarily wondering if I had actually survived the overdoses or if I was being kept alive in some sort of middle realm. I'd watched enough TV and read enough newspapers in jail to discover a lot of people over the last year hadn't been as lucky as I was. The fentanyl that had swept across America had engulfed many and demolished families and communities, yet I had stumbled out of the wreckage, mostly whole. Yet, the tattoos I was viewing was proof that I wasn't unscathed.

As the grip I felt began to loosen, I wondered if I'd be set free from wherever I was when I was able to finally expunge my demons. The ones that inked the hideous marks on my body. I had done a lot of 'soul searching' in that cell during the previous seven months before my sentencing day arrived. "This is no purgatory. We're going to make it out of here." I spoke and convinced myself now looking commandingly into the mirror at my own reflections.

I reached into where my razor was being pushed around at the bottom of the stainless-steel sink. I knew tomorrow was a big day. I knew it was the day my current path would be chosen. I knew full well it was 'sentencing' day. I went back to cutting my hair I'd let grow long since coming into County Jail. I had only taken a break to scope out my tattoos and recall the stories each one held, then back to cutting my hair. It wasn't an easy feat with the single blade razor and the plastic mirror, but I made do. Other options didn't exist in jail.

I didn't have much in the cell I could call my own. The few books were some of my only possessions. One of the books was the Bible I'd pulled from my nightstand; the one Father Peter had given me. Like the Tupac song, I'd found motivation in it. I knew I had now gone much further into it than the few sentences I'd read in my room the day I rediscovered it. The day the DEA raided me. In fact, it had now become my 'lifeline'.

I had been forced to do something I hadn't done in a very long time, confront myself. I had attended Narcotics Anonymous once a week in my jail pod. I'd been introduced to a word I'd heard before but had never dreamed about calling myself, 'addict'. "Hi, my names Cody and I'm an addict," I'd said it because I felt I had to. Everyone else was, so I fell in line with the others. Only later, alone in my cell did I process the claim and attempt to understand its complexity. "Hi, my name is Cody and I'm an addict," I'd said it to myself in the very mirror I was currently looking into while cutting my hair. This new title I'd given myself, I wanted to know about what it meant to be an addict. "Why am I an addict?" This question I couldn't answer. Not even with the help of my Bible.

I'd scoured the scripture to no avail, no real success. This had led me to believe there was no answer to my question. Nothing concrete stood out to me. I was searching for answers to something I didn't know the first thing about, addiction. I tapped the razor against the sink, cleaning it out. I was hurrying. The officer would be by in fifteen minutes to collect the razor under the door.

After dinner, I went back up to my cell to lay down and process the events that would unfold in the morning, on 'sentencing' day for my conviction. I wasn't nervous anymore; a calm had come over me. I'd replayed the scenario in my head so many times it had now been oddly comfortable as I lay there staring at the ceiling, my thoughts at ease. Or so I thought. I fell asleep.

I had dreamt, once again, of the jail pod I lived in and of the array of people that occupied it. Nothing spectacular, nothing a dream should be. Rest was all it was, nothing extra. As I laid on my bunk staring at the pages of my book, I recalled a conversation with an older man that had been my first cellmate months prior. When I initially came into jail, he had told me, "Enjoy your street dreams' while you still got them." At first, I had no idea what he was saying, but then I began to understand later when my 'street dreams' went away and became replaced with these new ones. I quickly understood what the man had been referring in saying 'street dreams'. Dreams of loved ones. Dreams of the life you used to know with the people you used to see. A world you used to occupy. Now replaced with dreams of jailhouse tiers and orange jumpsuits. White cinderblock walls, plastic mirrors, and stainless-steel sinks. That's what I had dreamt of last night. A constant reminder I'd been incarcerated for a lengthy duration already. We all had them, and we didn't talk about it. Occasionally if you were lucky an old memory still holding on deep within the recesses of your brain would become dislodged and you'd have the most wonderful sleep. The most wonderful dream. A 'street dream'. Last night wasn't one of those nights.

"Klunk!" a loud popping noise that signaled the unlocking of the cell doors radiated throughout the pod. I had been awake for quite some time, finishing another John Grisham I'd been lucky enough to obtain. Once a month a book cart was rolled into the unit. Its arrival immediately initiating a grudge match for the best books. The books were my window out of the reality I lived in, the other inmates could relate. Once a month they all scrambled toward the book cart. I placed the book on my tightly made bed and stepped out of my cell with a nervousness I hadn't envisioned myself having. With as many times as I'd replayed the day in my head, I thought I was ready. I stepped into the flow of inmate traffic going down the upper tier to the breakfast tables and a rolling carrier of food trays waiting for me and the other inmates. "Meals on Wheels," they called it.

I sat at my familiar table, one near the TV. It had required the use of a certain amount of seniority to infiltrate, which I had. "What's up Jason?" I asked Jason sitting across from me. "Not much." Jason replied, "You ready for your big day?" I spoke out "I thought I was last night but I'm kind of nervous now, you want my food?" offering my tray to my friend, unable to stomach it. As I sat and conversed with Jason, I couldn't help but glance to my left at the other inmates in the adjacent pod. Looking through the glass wall, the only thing separating the two pods, mine and his. Architectural torture for me if there ever was. I had been forced to watch him every day. He wasn't allowed to be in my pod, and I was glad. "He'd caused all of this," I thought. It was the friend that had 'wired up' and provided the audio from that last 'buy' that had been so incriminating. The audio that had tied me to the Federal indictment of 'Conspiracy', the charges I was soon to be sentenced for. I had been seething about him for months. "By the way, nice haircut," Jason said as I broke my seething stare from the old friend in the next pod. My now ex-friend.

Jason walked the two trays to the rolling food cart and re-joined me at the table. Now just a couple of hours from sentencing, my nervousness grew. The butterflies in my stomach, proof that I was in fact not as ready as I previously thought. "Lanus, you have a skype visit in 20 minutes," the officer who was running the pod barked. I looked at Jason across from me and shrugged my shoulders. "I wonder who that'll be?" I asked.

The first thing I saw as the skype screen came to life was Teddy's face, Lauren's childhood teddy bear. I remembered the ragged bear quite vividly from the days we had dated. The next thing I noticed was Lauren popping her head around the bear's weathered face. I smiled in the small cubicle that held the screen I was viewing. "Me and Teddy just wanted to let you know we'll be at your big day, and are wishing you the best of luck," Lauren said from behind the teddy bear still occupying the majority of the screen. She was waving the bear's hand as if Teddy were saying hello. I played along like I had when Lauren and I were together. "Hello Ted," I chuckled under my breath. A laugh, something so rare and elusive for me in this jail. "My mom's coming too, she wouldn't miss it for anything." Lauren continued. My smile, still unable to leave my face. I couldn't believe Lauren had continued to remain loyal to me, despite all I had put her through. These thoughts had consumed me during my county jail time, the thoughts of those relationships I'd hurt. The bridges I'd burned, there were many and I knew it. Finally, being made aware of it. A reality that was hard to live with alone in my cell, this weight I carried. "I'm so happy to hear you guys are coming," I responded.

Lauren and I chatted until the screen advised us, we had a couple of minutes remaining. I felt a sudden urge to say something. I didn't know what ignited it, but like most things, I went with it. "And one more thing," I said still looking at Lauren and the teddy bear on the screen. "What's up?" Lauren asked. "I'm sorry for all I put you through," I said, but more importantly I really felt it. The feeling that had come with the apology was something I had never experienced. Awkwardly enough, a high in itself. It felt good to me. "Me and Teddy forgive you," Lauren replied. What Lauren had said, it felt even better. I waited a few minutes before I left the small room. I didn't want the other inmates in the pod to see I'd been crying.

After the video visit, I felt the urge to prepare something to say to the courtroom. I knew the judge would ask me if I had anything to say. Hurrying, I scribbled some words on paper to read to my family and friends. I finished it just in the nick of time. "Lanus, let's go." the officer barked from across the pod.

As I entered the courtroom handcuffed in my orange jumpsuit, I knew the voice that was once again trying to speak to me. One that had been pretty insistent in my drug-using days. I knew she would be attempting to plant another lie. Yet now, I knew she was wrong. I smiled internally with that thought, and the thought that she was no longer gargantuan in my mind, but small and frail. I knew I was growing myself, internally. Becoming able to recognize her lies. I wasn't exactly where I wanted to be, but I was definitely growing. I knew this further with my ability to shut the voices off and read the letter I'd prepared to the courtroom.

"Do you have anything to say to the courtroom before I sentence you?" the judge asked me after reading the final charge I was now convicted of, Conspiracy to Distribute Fentanyl. I turned around looking at the small crowd that had assembled, my family and friends. As promised Lauren and her mom Gina were there. "Can I pull a letter from my pocket?" I asked the small team of U.S. Marshalls also sitting behind me. They nodded. I slowly reached into my pocket and pulled the letter out, unfolding it. I looked at the words I'd scribbled in the pod after my video visit with Lauren. I took a deep breath, but my hands were still shaking.

"I'm not exactly sure what to say, but I do know it starts somewhere with an apology to everyone that's here today. To my family and friends, to all those that were impacted by my reckless drug use and selling--I've hurt many." I began sobbing uncontrollably as the courtroom looked on, waiting for my next words. I waited a minute to gather myself before beginning. "You've got this Cody, I told myself over and over in my head. "Make your Dad proud," I told myself. I looked up for a moment and noticed the tears also falling from those that had come to watch me be sentenced. "I don't know if I even deserve one, but I hope everyone finds it in their hearts to give me a second chance. I hope everyone finds it in their hearts to forgive me." I fought the voice and read my letter to the courtroom. The judge then went to work to do his job. After the reading of the counts, he handed down a 12-year sentence in Federal Prison. Something I didn't really hear at first, 12 years, as my adrenaline was still pumping from the letter I'd just read. It had taken an immense amount of courage for me to read it, and after fighting through the tears, I had done so. It was a big victory nobody saw the way I had. Snapping back into reality with the memory of hearing "12 years" and the Marshalls pulling me from behind the desk I was standing at with my lawyer, I immediately asked, "Can I hug my Dad and say goodbye to my family and friends?" The Marshalls responded, "You can say goodbye, but you can't touch them." I looked toward my father, and he made direct eye contact with me. That second, we locked eyes. His blue eyes piercing through my green ones, about the only thing that wasn't identical to us. My entire life might be culminating in this seemingly sad moment, but it wasn't. Even at a distance, I could smell the familiar scent of my father. The Iowa air from the small town I'd visited so many times as a child. The memories returned to me. I could hear the swing in my grandma's backyard moving back and forth, a steady creaking. I could hear my sisters laughing and challenging me to "Go higher Cody!" Those 'every other' weekends and the 'childhood' I'd searched endlessly to understand were flashing before me. I could hear my Grandma yell one more time, "Slow down Cody." My life, was in that moment as I looked at my Dad, coming to the clearest understanding it ever had. "We'll be with you the entire way," Dad spoke up. The drug addiction had kept me in those moments as a child, but now the small boy in my grandma's backyard was vanishing. The small boy I had still been through my drug addiction, a child. In that moment, looking at my Dad, I finally grew. I was in that very moment be-coming what I always wanted to be, a man.

I didn't want to go back to my lonely jail pod or my cell. I wanted to hug the people I loved. "Come on, time's up," the Marshall's barked impatiently. My eyes erratic, a frenzy of back and forth amongst the commotion of people. I was trying to get one good look at every-one's face before my journey into Federal Prison. I knew I wouldn't see them for a long time. I caught a glimpse of Lauren and her mom Gina; they had kept true to their word, they were there. Their eyes, red and watery just like mine, an emotional day for everyone. As I was pulled backward by the Marshall's, Gina attempted to show off a written tattoo she had, all while speaking it out, "Piu all Storia." She was holding up her wrist and pointing to where she had been inked. No skulls or demons, but simply some words accompanied by a cross and two birds taking flight.

Seeing in my face the confusion of the foreign language of her tattoo and what she was yelling, Gina switched to English saying, "There's more to the story." As I was being pulled away by the Marshalls, "It means 'There's more to the story'," she yelled again. Now turned away from the crowd I was leaving with what she had said, "There's more to the story." Yet I was leaving with much more, the belief that what she really meant by the tattoo was, "There's more to 'My' story!" It was with that thought I took the first steps on my now 'time decided' journey.

12

'FEDERAL' A TASTE OF DIRECTION

Fifteen of us piled out of the cramped van and walked towards the looming building in front of us. The sound of our chains clink-clanking, the only noise allowed to fill the fall air. I was thankful to be out of County jail and even more thankful to be out of that cramped van. We were men packed in like sardines, filling the van to capacity. Hours earlier, when we initially got into the van, we all knew we shared the same nagging question. The one that every transferring Federal inmate asks themselves, "What prison will I end up in?" As we traveled away from the County jail the road signs began to give us all a pretty good indication of our fate. When the castle-like structure known as 'Leavenworth' appeared in front of us it was certain. With the curiosity now gone, all of us were equally terrified. We could only gawk at the stone fortress.

As I stared at the building of lore, I just could not believe I was here. I wasn't quite sure what Gladiators felt like going into the coliseum, but I now felt I had a pretty good idea, nervous to say the least. My stomach turned as I looked up at the gun towers. "Welcome to 'Gladiator School' gentlemen, aka 'The Hot House', aka 'Leavenworth'," the guard yelled from behind us. We had graduated from the County Jail of Jr. High School to the big leagues of High School Federal Prison. With it came the sick feeling of knowing there was no chance of turning back.

I knew I felt this churning gut feeling before, or at least one similar to it. Not long ago testosterone, and sweat, nervousness and bravery had brought it on within the realm of college football. Not to this degree, but I'd felt it. My closest association with such a situation as this. We continued shuffling in single file towards the gates. Clink-clank, Clink-clank, the chains between our legs hitting the hard concrete sidewalk.

My eyes shifted from the gun towers to the beaming sun, I couldn't help but stare at it. The sting in my eyes, the burn slightly satisfying. I hadn't seen its beauty for months and despite the pain in my eyes, I had a hard time looking away. Finally, I pulled my eyes from the burning ball of gas as the noise of a chain-link fence rolled across the pulleys, snapping me from my trance. The time to go in had arrived.

We piled into a holding cell containing other inmates. "Another van had arrived earlier," I deduced. None of us made eye contact with each other as we entered. This reflexive move was a primal regression that had occurred in the months we were locked up in County. It was now being transferred to this cell as we entered it. None of us wanted to be here and something as minimal as eye contact could send another man into a frenzy and we all knew it. The staring at the floor proved it. This tension, associated with caged animals. "Do not look them in the eyes," was all I thought as I found a spot to lean on the cold concrete.

The silence was interrupted by the first man brave enough to use the restroom after such a long trip. Soon, the constant flushing of a toilet now echoed through the concrete box we occupied. One by one we emptied our bladders, relearning the mechanics of it while cuffed and shackled in our jumpsuits. As I finished up, I couldn't help but notice the montage of graffiti etched into the concrete partition. Names of many men that had come before me. Names of men that were probably still inside Leavenworth's walls.

During County, every inmate going into Federal Custody calculates their perceived 'custody level', their 'risk level' so to speak, to gain insight into their possible destination. Hoping and praying for prisons located near them that they could potentially call home. With the help of my lawyer and other inmates, I had discovered the number to be around 7. According to the Bureau of Prisons, anything under an 11 is considered eligible for the lowest level, 'Camp Custody'. "So why am I in Leavenworth, a prison where inmates with much higher custody points are sent?" I thought as I crouched against the concrete wall. "I shouldn't be here. I'm a first-time, non-violent offender." But then again, nothing at this point would have surprised me. Feeling 'submitted' and 'defeated' at the same time, I wondered to myself, "How much worse can things get?" The indictment and withdrawals. The sentencing of 12 years and 'County' time, now Leavenworth. A new rock bottom had been found. One I thought couldn't get much deeper after the DEA had confronted me that day in the gym. I had been wrong though and was now discovering that the bottom is relative and 'going deeper' can always be found, no matter where I am, including Leavenworth.

As I stood there in thought, sulking, and questioning how I ended up in Leavenworth the holding cell door opened. An officer took one step into the room and barked an order "I need inmate Lanus, 17632030," as all the men looked up in unison. I was quickly pulled from my thoughts of self-loathing and gloom. As I stood to my feet, I was prepared for anything at this point and now convinced they had a special cage somewhere in a hole reserved especially for me, away from light and away from humanity. There I'd lay and wait out my sentence with a steady diet of moldy bread and putrid water occasionally thrown in. Clearly, I had gone mentally south. "Yes sir," I replied stepping forward. All eyes in the room were now on me as the situation unfolded. "You're my 'Camper', come with me." he continued. In a flash, my prayers had been answered. I now knew I wouldn't be going deep 'inside' Leavenworth.

I stutter-stepped forward; my feet not yet wired to full capacity due to the new 'Camper' emotions running through me. I stepped away from the large crowd of men and followed the officer down the hall and into a separate holding cell. I immediately knew what the officer had meant by calling me a 'Camper' and I knew enough to contain that excitement in front of the other men who were headed in the opposite direction. Otherwise, the exit from them might get ugly.

I left the men I had spent several months with in County and just like that, I knew I'd never see them again. They would be forced to endure the 'Gladiator' role without me. My internal excitement was unexplainably followed by an immediate pang of cowardness. "You're soft," a voice in my head whispered. "Be thankful you were saved because I had you right where I wanted you," the voice continued. The officer pointed to an open room and instructed me to go inside. Then he did something that solidified I had been through the worst of it. That my journey was only going up from here. Now, a climb from the bottom. A non-verbal queue that things were indeed looking up. Amazingly, for the first time since I had left the Sentencing Court, the Officer didn't lock the door behind him when he left!

In the quiet openness of that unlocked room, in the solitary of that space, I hit my knees and wept as quietly as I could, knowing there was somebody to be thanked.

A few hours later an officer entered the room and asked my pant and shirt size. Returning with a pair of 'green khakis', the camp color of clothing, I quickly changed. The men in the holding cell I had left would be receiving 'brown khakis', the color of clothing associated with higher risk, higher custody inmates. "Come with me," the officer said. As I left the room and walked back towards the door I'd arrived through, I passed the holding cell filled with the men soon to spend their first night in the real deal of Leavenworth. I put my fist up to the glass as I passed to a man I had grown to know in County. I stared at his arm sleeve of tattoos as he put it up to the glass. His hand forming a fist. We pounded each other through the glass and nodded. "Stay strong man," I mouthed as I continued following the officer.

I reached the rolling gate realizing the sun was now much lower in the distance. "Camps down the hill and counts in 30 minutes. Don't be late," the officer said closing the rolling gate as I stepped onto the other side. The officer walked away, and I remained frozen. Once again looking at the outer walls of Leavenworth. The fall air nipped across the flat Plains of the Midwest only to be stopped by the stones of Leavenworth rising up taller than any tree in sight. I turned into the breeze and started my trek down the hill to the camp. The outside air, an unexplainable feeling. I could see the smoke from the Camp rising in the distance. For the first time in the better part of a year, I wasn't wearing an orange jumpsuit, another unexplainable feeling. A new feeling was also upon me though and that was one I felt the most grateful to be experiencing, if even for a moment. A little dose of what felt like some semblance of freedom.

"What in the hell are you doing here?" the Camp's doctor barked at my intake appointment the next day. "I'm not sure I understand what you mean," I replied. "You're Ulcerative Colitis condition and bi-monthly infusions. We can't keep you here." the doctor responded. I had developed a condition called "Ulcerative Colitis" or UC during the last few years and had been on infusions since. "Well, we'll ship you out from here to the local hospital for them, however I'm putting you in for a transfer to a medical facility," the doctor continued. "So, you're saying I'm not staying here?" I asked. "That's correct," the doctor replied. "I'm sending you to a camp that's more suitable to handle your condition," he offered. I put my head down and sighed. Instead of seeing it as something positive my mind went negative. I simply wanted some stability. However, it would appear as if I'd be moving yet again.

I attempted over the next few weeks to gain insight from other inmates as to where 'medical camps' were located. I was told that there was only a couple in the United States, located on the coasts far from the Midwest. Furthermore, that most of the inmates who needed medical attention shipped from this area usually ended up in North

Carolina at a place called the Bunter Federal Medical Complex. "Hmm," I pondered when told. I'd never been to North Carolina before. My mind was once again a helter-skelter of uncertainties. So, I waited patiently until the day of my departure. That day would be just as uncertain as to my destination, despite all my guesses. I was beginning to understand how the Federal System worked.

"Why the green uniforms?" the nurse prepping my infusion asked. The Camp Driver, another inmate, sat with me in the infusion area of the Hospital the Leavenworth doctor had sent me. "We're on a landscaping crew," I joked. The nurse didn't buy it. She knew I was joking by the giggle erupting from my fellow inmate and I. "Seriously, what's up with the outfits," she persisted." I wasn't entirely prepped for this situation. "We're inmates at Leavenworth Camp," I replied.

She stopped what she was doing. Her jaw dropped and she appeared to be looking at us as if we were nuclear waste. Like something she shouldn't be handling. She silently started back up and continued her work of inserting the infusion needle into my vein and left the room. The inmate driver next to me just smiled. He frequently accompanied other inmates on these medical trips to the hospital downtown. "It never gets old," he laughed. "They always act like they've seen a ghost or something," he continued. My first taste of society's reaction to me as an inmate.

Despite her reaction, she soon returned. Even more surprising was her actions as she began pulling up a chair next to me. "I want to hear your story," she stated. "I want to know what you did," she continued. Nobody had asked me this before and I wasn't prepared to answer it. I certainly hadn't thought that this was how my day would be unfolding when I left that morning. "It's a long story," I said. "I've got time," she quickly replied. This nurse was persistent, and something appeared to be driving her to discover what was behind my conviction. I sighed and said what I thought appropriate for the circumstances. "I got in over my head with some Fentanyl," I replied looking the woman in the eyes. It was an abbreviated version with little detail. "Did you overdose?" she asked. "Twice, I overdosed twice. Why do you ask?" I replied. Tears formed in the woman's eyes. She pulled her red hair behind her ear with one hand and wiped the falling tear with the other. The Camp Driver and I looked on at the scene unfolding, not exactly sure how we should respond. Frozen we waited. "My son overdosed last month and is in outpatient rehab. He works in this hospital," she finally said through tears. She grabbed my hand and looked me in the eyes. The tears continuing to well. "Do you think you could talk to him?" she asked. "He doesn't work today but next time you get an infusion I'll make sure he's here. It would mean a lot to me," she finished. I looked at her in the eyes. A feeling of sympathy mixed with guilt stirring inside me. "Sure," I said. "I'll talk to him."

As the airplane full of convicts called 'ConAir' descended I could make out the tall pines below. Albeit great in stature they appeared as toothpicks from this distance. I had been taken first from Camp Leavenworth to the Oklahoma City Federal transfer facility. Leaving there I now was sitting next to a bulging U.S. Marshall, my head peeking over his shoulder to witness the landscape below. I was on a plane packed to the gills with Federal inmates and U.S. Marshalls. All soon to land in the state of North Carolina, or so we assumed. The inmates at Leavenworth had been correct in their deduction and prediction of where I would end up. The tires skidded as we rolled onto a runway filled with black SUVs and even more U.S. Marshalls. We would be taken by bus to my new home, the Federal Medical Camp in Butner, NC.

As I stepped off the bus, there was one thing I felt certain of, there was no way I would get through my prison sentence without getting more ink. The draw to tattoos remained for me addicting, and not to mention I found it a staple desire in the prison environment, along with other vices I was certain I would soon engage in. I was now happy to be in North Carolina receiving appropriate medical treatment because I was actually not happy that I had missed my tattoo appointment at Leavenworth. Just when I thought I could feel the sting of the needle enter my skin; I had been pulled from it.

The TV shows and movies had it right, prison ink was in no shortage. No matter how much the institution forbids it, it happens. At least that's what I'd seen so far. It was everywhere, and though I was not longer using, the temptation stirred inside me once again for tattoos. I wanted to finish the skulls. "Maybe I could find someone here, in this new place who could do it?" I thought. The risks were plentiful, but I didn't care. "If I'm going to spend several years in Federal Prison, I'm at least going to leave covered in tattoos!" I was convincing myself. The "Thug Life" mantra was still flickering around in my head. "Thug Life," I thought to myself as I found my way to my bunk. I was living it now, the Tupac song I seemed to have willed into existence, prison.

I threw my green duffle bag onto my bunk and took a seat, scanning my new surroundings. It was all the same, these prison camps: Humans packed into housing units, men sleeping on top of one another, community bathrooms with 5 showers and 5 toilets for

80+ men. Federal Prison Camp. Not to be confused with tents and smores or harsher conditions of other higher security prisons. Sure, there was less politics, but it was still prison in every literal sense of the word. Prison Camps. This one was just like Leavenworth. Neither one the kind of "camping" that sparks images of fishing and boating. I was sure the word would forever spark horror within me whenever mentioned as a free man again. I could see myself now. "Hey Cody, you want to go camping this weekend?" My mind flashing to the unit I now called home. This was not camping. It would be home for several more years though. This was closer to a tiny piece of the type of camping I'd read about in Germany than the kind I'd experienced as a kid in Iowa.

Early one morning the following week I heard my name over the prison loudspeaker which meant I'd be going, for the day, to the Federal Medical Complex up the hill on the prison compound. It was a 'high security' hospital that served a large number of medical needs within the Bureau of Prisons. Today was my first infusion day since arriving. As I walked to the front office to check-in and receive my departure instructions, I couldn't help but think of the nurse that had wanted me to talk to her son on this day back in Kansas City. "I want you to talk with him the next time you get an infusion," she'd said. Well, today was that day and I wasn't in Kansas City, I was in North Carolina. I hope he had completed his outpatient rehab his mother had told me about. I hope he was doing fine. I hadn't gotten to speak with him but "What would I even tell him anyway," I thought to myself walking to the officer's desk upfront. I had no cure. I had no prevention strategies or 12 steps I could offer. Nothing that the outpatient rehab place hadn't already taught him.

Besides, I wasn't even fixed myself. Matter of fact, I still wanted a fix, not to be fixed.

These prisons weren't designed as a place for the weak. Not for those attempting to kick habits, that's for sure. If anything, they were worse. I knew it was only a matter of time before I once again became victim to 'her'. The voice. I had nothing to lose anyway. I couldn't possibly mess things up any more than I already had. I became comfortable in the fact that I'd convinced myself, once again, that listening to her would be just fine. As I reached the officers I stopped all the convoluted thinking and handed them my ID.

"The bus leaves at 8 a.m. for the FMC" the officer barked. "Don't be late!" he continued as he handed the ID back to me after a cursory glance. As I walked to my housing unit, my mind became again trapped in the thought of 'ink'. "Tattoos. After I get the skulls done maybe I could finally get that sleeve I wanted. Maybe some more skulls. Maybe some roses. My mind was running wild with ideas.

I got back to the unit and took a lukewarm shower, a preset temperature I'd needed to get used to. Just hot enough to bear but not nearly hot enough to entice feelings of relaxation. Relaxation, that was another feeling I knew would become a fading memory in here. The water from my shower accumulated on the rusty pipes above my head, dripping back onto me in the form of rust water. It was a hell of a way to shower. Every so often you'd feel an unfamiliar drop and look down on your chest to see a brown spot disperse in the running water.

Semi-clean, I stood in my cell-like cubicle, cinderblocks forming 6ft high partitions. I was 6'3-1 could see everything. "Standing count.

Feet on the floor!" the officers yelled as they entered the unit. They walked by counting us like cattle. Humans being counted, I wasn't human anymore. "Humans don't get counted," I thought as an officer popped his head into my cube. "33...34" he murmured as he popped back out. I looked at my new cellmate and smiled. All we could do was make light of the catastrophe we'd found ourselves in, being counted.

As we stood in line for dinner, I recollected the last year: sentencing, county, Leavenworth, now this place. I was far from my family in the Midwest; however, my mom had recently relocated to Atlanta. She'd picked up and started over, again. She was decently close, within about 6 hours of driving time to the Raleigh area where I was.

As I stood there waiting for my food, I wondered if she'd ever come to see me. I wondered if my mother would even want to come and visit. If the last year had been a blur, the last 15 years had been just as crazy.

I peered outside at the medium-security prison across the street from the camp, the razor wire gleaming in the setting sun. Guard towers rising over both the camp and the higher security prison across the street. I didn't want my mom to have to come here and see me like this: green uniforms, a prison number stamped on my chest. This wasn't the condition a mother should see her son in. A pain ached within me, a pain signaling I didn't want food. I stepped out of the line and headed back to my unit to lay on my bunk. For the first time since college had ended, I picked up a pen and began journaling. I poured my feelings onto paper in my new home. It had sparked feelings within me. After journaling I went to the chapel to commandeer a new bible, the one Father Peter had given me had been confiscated.

I'd returned with not only a new bible but many books on many religions. Self-help too. I was loaded to the gills with books claiming they'd fix me. Like I had in County, I began feeling this gravitational pull to search out an answer. Why had I constantly thought I needed drugs? Tattoos? Now, Tony Robbins, Deepak Chopra, Rick Warren, Joe Vitale, and Jesus! Surely one of these men could provide me a suitable answer, a suitable resolution to my quandary.

13

THE STORY OF THE ROSE...

I entered my housing unit's ice room in some sort of apoplectic state from my severe cardiovascular workout and weightlifting that morning. The North Carolina sun was much different from the Midwest one I was used to. Much more unrelenting, stern in its ability to scorch human flesh. My sunburn, proof of that. The ice machine, a beacon in all its glory to relieve me. My throat was dry, and the feeling of cool thirst had overtaken me. Sweat still beading from my skin, no longer being contained by the paper-thin t-shirt I was wearing. My tattoos, visible through the dampened cloth. My sweat, dripping on the floor. A rhythmic 'drip-drip' of salt-water. My heavy breathing, much more recognizable in the close quarters of this room. The huffing and puffing of my lungs, heard only between the dispensing of ice, Clunk-ka-Clunk-ka-Clunk-ka-Clunk. The ice filling my cup was deafening in this tiny room. Yet there he was.

Hovered over the rickety desk crammed into the corner. His papers and books lining the tables. His Bible, it was all there. You get into the habit of brushing off the odd ones in prison. The Outliers. A man who thought this room a necessary workplace most definitely was one of them. "Weird,", I thought. Yet, I could not ignore the fact that he had recently given me some decent insight to ponder.

BEGINS IN CONFRONTATION...

Two weeks earlier in a different location I had questioned, "Who is this brave soul who dares come into my area?" 'My' area. The back of the kitchen was the cook's terrain. 'My' terrain. It would appear he had wandered from his lowly area in the 'tray room' to warm up a cup of coffee in the microwave. He had meandered into the den of a lion unaware of his mistake. He had no jurisdiction here. "Was he sick? Confused?" I thought. A bleeding seal in shark-infested waters, I gritted my teeth. There were only ever two ways to handle this type of situation. The rules must be established. Confront it or don't. Ignoring the latter, I took a step in his direction. It was the old man from my housing unit that came alive early and daily to occupy the ice room.

Before I could reach him on the other side of the kitchen, he had been confronted first by another kitchen worker. Another 'Bible Beater'. Not to be told about the rules, however, they were both discussing religion. Apparently, they both attended church together. I listened in as the words of "Christianity", "God", and "Jesus" were tossed around. I laughed as I folded my hands to my chest. "Inmate Christians," I pondered. The hypocrisy amusing. "Never trust an inmate Jesus Freak." As I pretended to occupy myself, I listened to their conversation and thought of Kayli.

The world seemingly in her hands. A beautiful girl, a beautiful soul. I had met her in college. She had dated one of my best friends and that friend had just informed me that she had taken her life. An email that had shaken me. She'd succumbed to a hideous demon, depression. A demon I'd seen and recognized. A demon I was still fighting while locked up in this prison. I had questions, none of which this "God" or "Jesus" character had ever answered. Seething for answers it was time to approach this old man who'd wandered into my kitchen, who'd brought these feelings erupting to the surface with his Jesus talk?

I hit him with it, a sucker punch I knew he wouldn't expect. I was never one to hide the words I felt, and this man was about to experience it firsthand. "I had a good friend just commit suicide. Where is she, Heaven or Hell?" I bellowed at him. The question didn't need sugar-coating; I didn't care about his readiness. "If he knew his stuff, he'd have an answer," I thought. "And don't tell me what I want to hear. What do YOU believe?" I barked. I had placed him in a lose-lose situation, and I had been glad to do it. He was in my area, not his. I knew he wouldn't be able to produce a satisfactory answer and I'd gladly bounce him out of the kitchen, never to return. The other kitchen worker standing by in awe of the situation unfolding before him. I took a step towards the Old Man, our eyes meeting. He, seemingly unafraid, took a step towards me. Our eyes remained locked. A standoff. He then began to speak.

...YET PROGRESSES

After filling my cup with ice, I debated about chatting with him again. I had enjoyed his insight the previous week. I took a step in his direction and grabbed a chair from the stack in the corner.

As I set the ice room chair next to the Old Man he looked up from his work. "Hey Gary, I appreciate your answer in the kitchen the other day. I know it was out of 'left field', but I just wanted to let you know I appreciate it," I said. "No Problem Cody. Hey, I was hoping we could chat more on what we discussed," he said. "I'm glad you stopped by," he continued. He pulled out a notepad and began drawing ten rose plants starting from their infancy as a seed to their maturity as a full rose bush. I sat patiently sipping my water and watching as he drew. Sweat still dripping from my shirt onto the floor. "Have a good workout?" he asked as he finished the drawings. "It wasn't bad. Pretty hot out there," I replied. He pushed the paper over between us on the rickety desk and pointed at it. "Which one of these rose plants is a ten?" he asked. "Umm, do you mean which one is the best?" I replied. "Yeah, which one's the best if that is your definition of a 10", he continued. Studying the pictures, it didn't take long for the response to be conjured up. I pointed to the last bush, full and covered in roses. "That one," I said. I pointed to the rose I thought 'best', full and covered in flowers. It wasn't beautiful because the Old Man wasn't the best artist, however my mind had been able to envision them. "Women don't like just one flower," I thought to myself, "They want a dozen." My entire life I had been told that more was better, infatuated with excess in its entirety. In this world, it's better to have more than less, and I'm sure the Old Man would agree. More money. More muscle. Of course, the rose bush with more roses is a '10', I thought, my finger now pointing and touching the paper.

"You see Cody, you're wrong. That seed had the potential to be that rose bush the entire time. Matter of fact, the seed 'is' the rose bush. So, it's a ten just as well. And so, is this one. And this one. And this one." The Old Man was pointing to all the rose bushes he had drawn. He pushed the paper away and once again made eye contact as he had in the kitchen. "Kayli's a ten, you're a ten, we're all tens," he continued. "In God's eyes were not a seed or a rose bush. It doesn't matter the stage of life you're in. We're all the same to

God. Absolute tens," he finished. I rejected his answer and of course wanted to debate with him. "Gary, I'm far from a ten, man. I'm in Federal Prison. I've disappointed my parents. I've lost everything." I had given him a response he was ready to argue himself. "Things happen Cody and sometimes life throws us curveballs, wherein we make shitty decisions. At no point does our outward status ever change our inward beauty that God knows we possess. You know Cody, that rose bush seed looks like a million other seeds. But you know the difference between you and that rose bush seed? It knows it has the potential 'as' a ten from the very start. So, my question to you Cody is this. Do you know your potential started as a ten and remains a ten?"

"When you stop trying to 'be something' you already are and when you stop trying to 'find something that you already have, your life will change." Gary said this as he pointed to my chest, toward my heart.

As I thought about the potential power in what he said, if it were really true, something sparked inside of me. I could only stand as if paralyzed as the ice machine continued…. Clunk-ka, Clunk-ka, Clunk-ka, Clunk.

14

THE CALLING...

"Cody, just write your 'spiral into addiction' story out in a few pages," Paul said, "Maybe it'll gain some traction if you put it out on social media and we can get you pardoned." This man, for some crazy reason, would not let it go. I couldn't contain my laughter at what I was hearing. I doubled over, my palms on my knees. "You have got to be kidding me, Paul. That is the most ridiculous thing I've ever heard. A fentanyl dealer? A freaking fentanyl dealer? I'm the last person Trump would pardon," I replied. "What, can it hurt to try?" he asked as he continued his prison job of placing ketchup packets on three hundred trays before each meal. Bored, I was assisting him at the time by adding the mustard packets and together we prepared the trays for the infamous prison's 'hot dog day'. The inmates loved them. Returning from my laughter I said, "That should do it," as I placed the last packet on the tray and looked at Paul. His face, one that in a way surprised me because it revealed he was actually being serious and seemed genuine in wanting my story. "I'll think about it," I said walking back into the kitchen as a timer on the oven rang out in the background. "But don't count on it. It sounds like a ludicrous idea." I yelled over my shoulder knowing the tater-tots weren't going to jump off the pan themselves.

A few months passed, all the while Paul continuing to persist in getting my story. He was leaving in a couple of weeks and now had an added motive. He wanted some stories from inmates to gain attention on prison reform that he appeared to be contemplating getting involved in when he was finally out. He continued to beg me, almost daily, for mine. I had finally given in thinking "Screw it, why not." So, I had written out six measly pages to pacify him and put an end to the questioning.

What had really surprised me was how difficult it was to write it. It was my story; my life and it was difficult to put into words. From the very first, I began reliving the events now from my completely sober mindset. Unexpectedly, a tough task. My raw emotions pouring onto the paper. I had stayed up all night writing and well, crying too. It was crazy what had been happening to me as I wrote, as I relived the events that had led to my arrest. It was as if it was surreal, for sure. Despite the pain and sadness in reliving my story through the pen; that night as I wrote I actually felt the first easing of that very pain. Relief. Some barriers seemed to be breaking down. Strangely it was the need to experience more of that pain from my memory in order to receive relief in my current reality. It seemed a backward resolution for sure, but a resolution no doubt.

The words on the paper I now clutched in my hand portrayed that very process of resolution, I was certain. You could even make out some dried teardrops on the paper's edge as proof. Spots where the paper ruffled up like the bedsheets it was written from. Dried teardrops. All this was very personal, and I felt a bit embarrassed as I walked out of the back of the kitchen toward the nearly empty premeal dining room. I wanted to read it to Paul myself. If I was going to expose myself like this and tell my story, I wanted to be the one to read it first.

When I reached the dining room, I observed Paul having a conversation with another man at the table next to him, Gary. The guy who had been brave enough to walk into my Kitchen domain to heat up his coffee. The old man that had told me the story of the rose in the ice room. I paused, uncertain of how I should handle the situation. "Ask Gary to leave or just sit and read it to Paul anyway?" I pondered. I knew the old man was always about his own work at a table away from the raucous bantering of the other workers waiting for the shift to start. I figured that none of my stories would have any importance to him. I contemplated these things as I clutched the pages and slowed my pace to allow time to decide. As I approached the table a persistent voice in my head was telling me to turn away. "Why would you read your stupid story even to Paul let alone within earshot of Gary. Letting those two old men hear it is just going to embarrass you." And then, I did something I couldn't remember ever doing up until that point in my life. I ignored the voice, sat down, and began to read.

"There, are you happy?" I barked at Paul as I finished reading the story, still holding onto it dearly as if a prized possession. "Let me get a copy of that," Paul replied, his hand reaching out across the table. "Not a chance," I replied recoiling back with the paper. "It needs more work. I'll get you a copy before you depart," I adamantly said as I got up from the table. Gary hadn't said anything as we were a bit separated by the space between the two tables. But looking my way for a brief second, he had nodded with a slight grin indicating to me some sense of approval of what he might have overheard. He then turned and stared out the dining room window in front of his table. It seemed I had wanted him to hear it because at that moment I wanted words of encouragement and satisfaction not blank stares out a window. I felt a bit defeated in not receiving such from him as I headed back into the familiar territory, back into my kitchen domain. "Hey Cody," Gary said. My back to him and in midstride. I turned back to the table, to the old man who seconds ago was lost in some sort of trance. Gary's previous conversation with Paul having been interrupted by a lunatic with a ridiculous story of his trip into addiction, I could only imagine what was to come from him. "Good job on the story," he said. I looked at him. His words of approval minimal but genuine. Just enough to satisfy my craving for any kind of acceptance of what I'd read. I smiled at him and turned, continued walking back to the kitchen. The story still crumpled in my hands. "Thanks man," I yelled back.

As I rifled through my tiny locker looking for a pair of socks I watched as the story I had written a week prior fell out. Frozen, I watched as it leafed to the ground. My mind began to go back and forth with emotion as I was reliving the events of last week in my head as I looked at the papers laying on the floor of my cell. I picked them up and stuffed the story deep into the back of my locker and pulled out a pair of socks, closing the door only to be startled by an old man standing in my cell door. It was Gary. He was everywhere.

He said something funny as if a sailor as he stood in the doorway with one arm on the door frame. "Permission to come aboard?" At least he was being respectful of serious prison protocol to not step into another man's Cube without asking first. "Be my guest," I replied pulling up a chair and swiveling out the metal stool on the small steel writing desk. "Have a seat, what's up?" I asked as I sat facing him literally 2 feet away and pulling my socks on waiting for him to speak. Gary proceeded to tell me how much he had been moved by something I had said in my story that I had read to Paul. That he had then been motivated to talk to me about a project of his own. "I have this story I've been interested in helping bring to light," he said. "And you just might be the right fit for it." he continued. My mind began to spin with "First Paul with his ideas, now Gary." This is getting out of hand. "What in the hell is going on," I thought to myself pulling on the last sock and sitting up. "What kind of story?" I asked. "It's a story about tattoos," he replied. "A story about an antidote in the evolution of getting tattooed," he continued. "I've been praying about a man that would be willing to write a story surrounding every one of his tattoos. What was his motivation? Why the timing of it? What caused him to choose that particular tattoo? What was he hoping to say by it? That sort of thing."

Here I was staring at a white man in his 60's that I would be willing to bet not only didn't have any tattoos visible or hidden anywhere but quite possibly never contemplating getting inked at all. Here he was asking me if I wanted to write about tattoos. So naturally out from my mouth came "What's your angle on such a book?" He seemed ready and eager to reply. "See Cody, when I am released, I am called to put together a company that will from time-to-time feature books that I believe will have an impact on people's lives physically, mentally, emotionally, and spiritually. I have been studying and listening to stories over the last 6 years in prison of the many reasons surrounding why men get tattoos. I believe there is an element of it that is not being exposed in a single tattoo event. Yet, it can be revealed by hearing of how they evolve, over time, within a man's mind and on his body. I would like that hidden element to be exposed and feature it as one of the books someday. I know this is a lot to ask and I just jumped you with it, so take some time and think about if you would like to even write about your tattoo experiences."

"Why me?" I snapped a bit puzzled.

"After hearing something quite profound in your story that I over-heard you read to Paul last week, I was instantly pricked to believe that you may well be the very person to write such a book."

I told him I would think about it and let him know soon. He was thankful and left me to my thoughts saying "Cody, just know that I will respect whatever your decision is, without explanation, so no pressure from me, ok?" I nodded affirmatively as he turned and left.

I cannot yet explain the 'why' of what happened next, but I did it, nonetheless. Literally, two minutes after he left my cube, I was standing in front of his, asking permission to enter. I had come to deliver my decision. I had two words for him which I spoke, shook his hand, and left before he could even respond.

'I'm in!"

So, the days had turned to weeks and the weeks to months. The weather from cold to almost bearable. Paul had left without the story he wanted, the one I had stuffed into my locker. I soon be-lieved in its new purpose. I was soon convinced by Gary that the story could quite possibly have a more impactful journey within the lives of those who read it. For me something quite possibly much bigger than a pardon by a president. Imagine that? It had grown significantly larger in scope and drive as the days passed. I began meeting with Gary over the book he believed so dearly in. From weekly to daily to many times during a single day we met. The discovery of my voice in the stories surrounding each tattoo and of my journey into the world of drugs and addiction in between them was now driving me to the same belief. Then one day Gary asked out of the blue as he sat facing me in the ice room, "Cody, have you discovered the 'antidote' to your drug addiction within your stories yet? The real lasting NARCAN of addiction?" Taken a bit back by the questions as if he were implying that I was still an addict I snapped forcefully back "I'm all done with that Gary, I don't 'want it' anymore! I'm not worried about my future in that area!" What he said next would further enflame me. "Not 'wanting it' is not enough and it is not the 'antidote'. Having it be absolutely 'not necessary' for your life is. And it is the 'antidote' that you will discover that will get you there. He remained calm in expressing his assertiveness that he held the truth. I was getting loud and heated in expressing my own truth during the back-and-forth exchange and it pissed me off to the point that I left. Yet, the ringing in my mind of all that was said refused to leave. A few days later I picked back up my pen and began to write again. I was none the happier, but I was, if one thing, committed. I said I would write the book and I would. I knew something Gary did not know yet. He was dealing with Cody Lanus!

Then the day came when during a meeting over the book I knew it was time for me to confront him. I had been thinking hard over it since our latest Ice Room Exchange.

"Listen Gary, you leave soon, and I have no clue what the antidote is. How in the hell am I supposed to write about something I don't even know exists?" I spoke. Another session beginning with me red in the face, another chapter had been written, and another failing to allow me to recognize 'The Antidote' Gary kept on informing me I would discover. "You'll find it, Cody. I'm sure of that," he replied. "Keep searching," he continued. I threw my arms up in the air feeling once again frustrated and defeated. "Ugh, whatever man!" I replied. Gary once again just calmly set there across from me at the table in the recreation room we so often occupied for our night meetings. Smiling!

And so, he left. He was set free. I remained behind with the story of my life that had grown immensely on paper from its inception. Many more pages past the measly six I had read to Paul and over-heard by Gary way back on that day in the prison cafeteria. I hadn't discovered that elusive 'antidote', but I had slowly begun to discover something else, myself. I was revealing both the voice and the voids. Those things that had driven my drug use, I discovered them. That darn antidote though, non-existent. The thing Gary claimed would eventually come. He left me with my story and a sealed envelope holding a letter from him. He left convinced that the 'antidote' for my addiction story was near and would soon be discovered. Being not convinced and pained I took the sealed envelope and the begin-nings of the book and stashed them both back into the darkness of my footlocker. There were a few reasons I wasn't eager to rip the en-velope open. Reasons only an inmate watching a friend leave prison while he remains 'inside' can explain. I knew those words within the envelope, whatever they were, to be Gary's last to me for quite some time. I'd wait to pull the envelope out when I hit another wall, when

I was having a bad day. Maybe they'd inspire me then. Maybe they'd pull me from the slump I would find myself in on that particular day. For now, in my mind, it would sit and rest as another jailhouse book that would not be finished was stashed away. Another big idea that would never come to fruition. Closing the locker, I thought "Maybe I'll pull it out again and write some more someday. Maybe I'll read what's in the envelope too someday. Maybe someday I'll discover the antidote too." I continued as I snapped the padlock shut on my footlocker. "But not today. Today I've got 'prison time' to do!

15

THE LOGAN EFFECT

COINCIDENCE...

It had been a frustrating day, to say the least. Lots of things can go wrong in this prison environment and today they had. My Wednesday morning workout ritual was first delayed due to the locked exit door from my housing unit. Once finally freed from that I stood in front of the second locked door of the day, the prison's recreation room door and coarsely thought, "This is the story of my life lately!" Tap, tap, tap; my foot was hitting the concrete. This had become an automatic response to my inability to handle the reasoning of this obstacle that was laid out in front of me, a correctional officer who simply didn't feel like getting up to unlock the door. As each minute passed, I could feel my anger growing. My workout was now in jeopardy of being delayed another two hours. An inmate 'census' count was approaching requiring me to return to my bunk, ultimately pushing things back even further. My routine, 'MY' routine! Locked doors, counts, restraints of all kinds! My life as an inmate was being defined by my ability to handle these routines, restraints, and limitations. A virtual thumb on my back. Today I was clearly struggling with it. These are small things to the free man, yet mountains to a prisoner. It might as well have been Everest to me at that moment. Only supplemental oxygen would make it surmountable. This feeling I had as I got 'angry' began circulating in my stomach. I attempted to subdue it with positive self-talk and positive imagery. The very self-control strategies I'd relied on time and time again. Then I slipped. "Why couldn't they just unlock the doors on time?" I thought to myself. "Why the hell is everything such a pain in the ass around here?" The countless self-help books I engulfed myself in were not helping in the least at that moment. They were now just books, read and forgotten by me. I was sensing that all the motivational big wigs couldn't pull me out of this one. I mentally searched for a tool Tony Robbins would use in this situation. To no avail, it wouldn't come no matter how hard I tried. Finally, completely pissed, I stormed back to my cell from the rec building, kicked my shoes off, and jumped up into my bunk. I dug my face into my pillow and couldn't stop what came next. I cried. This place, this life I was now living. I was allowing it to tear at me. Two years of this under my belt and I thought I would have better control by now. But I didn't. My emotions, a tornado, spiraling out of control, I continued crying. I felt like an infant. My mind went deep. "He was gone." It was the old man, Gary that came to mind. I knew a time like this would come and here it was. I needed his words, his motivation, now. As if instinctively, I hopped down from my upper bunk and grabbed the letter from my locker he had written to me when he left a month before.

Holding the unopened envelope that held the letter, memories of the man I had befriended flooded over me. Since he'd left writers' block' had overcome me. I was infected with the inability to write and I had stopped the story. I just wasn't sure where it should continue, so I didn't. He was gone, the old man I once thought righteous. He had become much more than that though. Through the process of laying my story on paper, I'd confided a lot of my life to him. Now gone, I wasn't sure what to confide in. He'd grown to be a friend. The Monday 'Book' meetings, my therapy sessions of sorts I had looked forward to, gone. The guidance I needed to put this story on paper, gone. The tears in my eyes, proof of our bond, real. Now holding the letter, it was the only thing I had left of him. He was now a free man, and I was genuinely happy for him. It is an un-explainable feeling you can't appreciate until you've experienced it, a prison friend getting set free. Prison is tricky, with lots of moving parts you're not supposed to understand, yet they happen anyway. One day someone is here and one day they're not. A simplicity that's terrifying as it is artless. "I hope he's ok," I thought as I clutched the letter. "I hope the world hasn't sped up too much for him." Then my mind somehow formulated something that had remained dormant within my writer's block, "We have so much more to talk about, so much more to write," as if speaking to him directly. Yet, as I set there, I couldn't hide my jealousy, my envy in his freedom. I wiped the tears from my eyes, tore open the envelope and began reading the letter he left me.

2019 / 4.17
Cody!

What a ride! And to think it's just begun! Wow! the good Lord knew what he was doing when he orchestrated our connection! You have been masterfully obedient to the call! Proud of you, my man.

I am not lost to the magnitude of the task in a man digging deep! Most, and I mean most, will never have the fortitude. And they will never experience the reward that you will receive. It has begun for you already in the unfolding of the journey. I have seen it in your demeanor and spirit. Someday others will see it "Live"!

And when that occurs it will be a new and special achievement for you because you will not be doing it to fill a painful 'void' but to fulfill the destiny of the "Rose"! The rose you always were, are now, and always will be! You don't' have to look anymore for something that is already you. You just need to let the nutrients of life and the light from "above" blossom you! Remember this when the mind and others try to have you think otherwise. I am blessed, surely blessed, to have been chosen to be a part of your journey. And I look forward to myself being obedient to what I am called to do to go with you to the finish line, which will then be your next starting line! See, I already know you pretty well! "Don't stop now" I hear you saying!

I have enclosed a letter I put together for a former inmate who struggled with his family similar to the struggle with yours. I could only share with him how I dealt with it through my own conse-quences. The release from it is what allows 'You' to be at peace, un-burdened by its awful hold. I trust you will know the time to put it to good use. I will keep you in prayer as you build a new relationship with your family.

All things are possible with God. Go to him for strength and guidance in that path. He will not let you down. You are a Holy Spirit filled man and you can control the height of its flame in your heart. It is at the calling of your voice. Mastering that and its power to fulfill your life will astonish you. I have great faith in you because I know God's got you. We really perform at our best when we per-form for the audience of "One". In that, the need to be validated by everyone else is gone. Then when others do cheer us on in the journey it's yes, sweeter, but not because we need it, but we realize they see what God sees already in us.

So, I will move on now to get in a position to make the next step possible. I will look forward to reconnecting soon! Remember my friend I am with you in spirit! Be good to you! Paced, focused, deliberate, and contemplative... Cody style!

God's Peace, Love ya Brother.
Gary

I thought of his words "…with you in spirit," as I put the letter down, finally feeling the regaining of my composure from the 'locked door incident'. The letter had been just what I needed. I was still holding the remaining pages, the 'Forgiveness Letter' he had enclosed. "So that's what he must have been talking about all that time. That thing to fill the voids, forgiveness," I tried processing it in my mind. "No way could 'forgiving' be the key to eliminate my voids, my drug addiction, the person I'd become," I questioned. "Prison has fixed me; I am certain of that. But I don't believe I have anyone to forgive or anyone I hold any animosity towards to forgive, so it can't be that, or can it?" my mind now in a scramble as if avoiding a conclusion. I didn't want to believe the letter. I wasn't ready to handle the possible weight of its contents. I wasn't about to accept that this is where the road had led. I found myself frazzled, wanting the dialog I was having with myself to stop. I jumped up and stuffed his 'Forgiveness letter' unread back into my footlocker. "I bet the Rec Room is open by now!" I thought as I bolted from my cubical. The letter, left behind padlocked in the darkness.

There it would remain for another two weeks as I continued in my mental paralysis. I had reached past it every morning and night to grab my toiletry bag, unable to bring myself to even touch it. The same thing was happening again this morning. It sat in the bottom staring back at me as I reached past it once again. Blowing it off mentally, I grab my bag. Closing my locker, I exited my cell and turned toward the hallway leading to the bunkhouse bathrooms. "It can wait another day," I repeated once again the twice-daily mantra. In the distance as I could just barely see the top of the community desk that was mounted on the right-hand wall. It was forever cluttered, always holding random items. An area that magazines and newspapers piled up or things other inmates had abandoned when leaving, were tired of, or just plain ran out of room in their tiny lockers. A common area, 'The Land of Misfit Mail and Newspapers'. My daily news came in the form of month-old New York Times and Wall Street Journals from that very spot. My connection with the happenings in the outside world came from this desk, these articles other inmates now deemed unworthy. I looked forward to my morning walk to the bathroom wondering what treasures may lie in this literary graveyard. Amongst the new stack of the material was a Sports Illustrated magazine from March 11, 2019, it was now May. It was the magazines titled "The Logan Effect ... Lives Lost, Lives Saved"* that caught my eye as I walked by now headed back to my cube. This time I reached down and picked it up. I stared at the cover picture that showed a number 27 jersey hanging from a hockey net. I had no knowledge at that time of this young man's story in Canada or the real 'why' of me picking the magazine up. To conceive or believe that it would inspire me to finish my story in North Carolina couldn't have and didn't enter my mind. "The Logan Effect" is all I whispered under my breath as I headed to the bathroom.

The article grabbed my attention with its first three words: "The Beloved Coach." Reading on it began introducing me to a man that Logan Boulet, a young hockey player from Canada, looked up to. The coach, Ric Suggitt, aka 'Sluggo'. A coach that the magazine described so perfectly that it was as if he was, in fact, a man that I knew. A man I felt I could see myself looking up to also. A man that incredibly reminded me of some of my great coaches in my days as a local sports hero. The ones that found joy in pushing me as a young man to reach my fullest potential. Logan Boulet, like many other kids, confided in a gregarious man that pushed him to obtain the 'Assistant Captains' title. Giving him the 'A', he had earned and worn so proudly on his Humboldt Broncos jersey. As I read on, the article showed where the first 'ripple' of the 'Logan Effect' had begun, the cerebral brain hemorrhage that would take his mentor Sluggo's life. He was just 58 years old.

...OR GODSCIDENCE?

As I put the article down, I couldn't help but think of the Coach I had lost at Northwest Missouri State. A coach in college that all of the players looked up to, Scott Bostwick. He died the same year I met Lauren. The same year I would move to Omaha. Logan's story had me thinking about my own story, the one folded up in my footlocker along with the 'Forgiveness Letter' Gary had left me. The letter I had yet to read. Tears were always hard for me to contain and in that moment, I felt powerless in my ability to hold them back. With my head down in an attempt to hide my tears, I continued thinking about Coach Bostwick, about Sluggo. "They certainly would have had a ton in common," I thought. "May they both rest in peace," I continued. Saying a quick prayer, I picked the article back up and dried my eyes. I continued reading.

Sluggo's heart continued beating despite the brain hemorrhage he experienced. An earlier discussion before his death solidified Jen's decision to donate her husband's heart after he died. In Canada, families can donate organs after death. "A life is lost, and a life is saved" so the call to the reason to begin the ripple effect. The ripple that Sluggo started had a huge impact on Logan. He became personally inspired to donate his own organs when he was old enough. He would later tell his Dad, Toby, that on his 21st birthday he wanted to become an organ donor. "Logan they're not going to want your organs when you're 80 years old," his dad with his hope for a long life for his son responded. "But go ahead anyway."

When that day came Logan held true and fulfilled his commitment, he signed his donor card. He was later asked if he felt it weird to think about his organs being cut out. "If I can save six lives, I'm going to do it," Logan would proudly respond.

The beginning of his own ripple would start just four short weeks later. A truck smashed into the bus carrying Logan and his team. A very tragic event that shook Canada hard, albeit the world. That day an intersection in rural Saskatchewan became littered with hockey debris and young men's lives. Among them was Logan. With seeing but a scratch on his head, a lump on his temple, and a cut on his big toe, the outward scan of Logan would reveal but minimal damage. Internally though scans would reveal much worse: a broken neck, a broken spine, and a massive brain bleed. Logan's critical care physician Joann Kawchuk would later say, after seeing what the scans reveal, that "Logan will not recover." His heartbeat though, like Sluggo's had, continued beating strong.

I went on to discover that sixteen people died at that intersection. As I continued reading through the article, I had to put it down several more times to regain my lost composure. People were passing by my cell, yelling my name. Some stopping inside to converse, asking mundane questions that I'm sure were to simply pass prison time. I realized I had been a newly incarcerated inmate at the Leavenworth Prison during the initial happenings of the Canadian accident. I had been unaware of this incident Sports Illustrated was now describing. To read it was as if it just happened the day before. The magazine was literally outlining the power of 'The Logan Effect' that had transpired at the one-year anniversary of the 2018 crash.

Logan's death was new to me and because I saw a little of myself in him, I felt like we'd known each other before. As he lay in a grave and I sat at my desk in my prison cell, questions began flooding over me. "Why would you save me, a drug addict?" I thought. "Why was I allowed to live and a promising young man like this and his teammates would be taken so young?" I continued asking these questions to God. I received no immediate response. I stared down at the team picture of the Humboldt Broncos, all the young men smiling after a win. The world ahead of them. I smiled as they smiled back. I looked even closer.

Logan in the front row, the 'A' on his jersey as clear as a Scarlett Letter. I looked away knowing the questions I was asking God wouldn't be answered. I stood up from my desk and pushed my toiletry bag back into my locker past the 'Forgiveness Letter', past the story Gary had inspired me to write. There it lay. Piled up in the back of my locker. A story I still believed since Gary's departure may never be told.

Logan's death and 'his' story of the Humboldt Broncos would gain international headlines. The organ donation story, a special gift in an organ 'donation stricken' country. Logan's story would inspire tens of thousands to donate their organs. A movement that had now grown into 'The Logan Effect'.

"What if my intentions grew into writing my story to help people like Logan had," I wondered. "To save lives as he did." I continued. "But my story is just another drug addict story, not like Logan's in the least." I pondered these ramblings as I closed the door to my footlocker. Then something Gary had said in his farewell letter popped into my mind and caused me to think, "What 'new' starting line had Gary been referring to?"

Sitting once again with the magazine I continued reading the article and discovered "Logan donated his heart, lungs, liver, kidney, pancreas, and corneas. Officials would later tell the family that all six transplants were successful, that all recipients were still alive." The wish Logan had made on his 21st birthday had come fully true. "He saved six lives," I whispered to myself.

As I was finishing up page 72 of the Sports Illustrated, I glanced over at the next page and sensed something I knew I would never forget, a coincidence of 'my' life. A message. It was in that instant I heard, "The ripples of the Logan Effect are still moving. Clearly, far out of Canada and right here into this Federal Prison Camp in North Carolina." That very next page I had glanced at was an Ad Article for 'Partnership.' Their slogan is what pulled my eye,

"Hoping can't help a kid struggling with drugs. But together we can." I laughed saying almost out loud "Aint that the truth!" The ad, sandwiched in between the pages of Logan's story said, "We partner with parents and families to get help for kids whose drug or alcohol use threatens their lives with addiction." Logan's story, my story! I was in awe. "Out of all the ads in the magazine why this ad? Why this spot?" I asked myself. I continued thinking this as the last word I'd read reverberated through my head...'Addiction'. Now this was something I knew all too well. This had to be more than a simple coincidence.

The similarities in our stories wouldn't stop there. The connections and parallels wouldn't stop either. Unlike my reasons to get my many tattoos Logan's friends and family would get tattoos of hockey sticks with Logan's initials. A different kind of motivation for getting them than I knew I had ever felt when walking into a tattoo shop. These people, Logan's people were not getting skulls flaunting death. These were tattoos inspired by a selfless choice. A choice manifested through the death of the very young man who made it. His choice causing a ripple effect that was now moving thousands to make the same selfless choice and donate not just organs, but life. I was completely humbled in my cell reading the powerful article. I found myself looking down at my own tattoos and once again posing the question to myself., "What were you thinking?" If I didn't despise them before knowing Logan, I sure did now.

This was an awareness I felt I needed to let myself feel; someone having a decent reason to get inked and my reasons.

Reading on, I discovered that Fiddler, the eyewitness to the Canadian bus crash uses one of the same names when she has dreams about the hockey players. Her appreciation of the life-altering event she witnessed. "They're my Guardian Angels," she says about the boys that died in that horrific crash. At that point I put the article down, it was getting too raw. In fact 'Lifesavers' and 'Guardian Angels' were things I had coined as the names for the two Narcan shots that had saved my life. As the darkness of my tattoos and my own story began to resurface, I knew I would have to finish the article later.

As I sat for a second in hopes of letting some of it settle, I recognized and decided to accept and say "This article was clearly meant for me to discover. Logan, his coach, my coach, the tattoos, the addiction ad, the Guardian Angels, all of it seemed to have come from a Higher Power." With that, another question came to me that I immediately directed toward God as I tried to process its implications. With Logan in mind, I asked, "What would he have wanted to tell his family before he died? What would he have wanted to tell himself? I'm sure he probably would have had a lot to say, had he known." I got up from my desk and grabbed my radio out of my footlocker. I needed some laps around the track to cool down. I needed air.

I stepped outside and felt the warm embrace of the sun. A feeling I no longer took for granted. County jail time will do that to a man, make him appreciate nature. The smell of the air, yes, it has a distinct smell. Something you don't notice until you notice it. A smell that existed all along. Free air circulating through the trees and over the dirt. All the things nature provides in a breeze. In a breeze on your face. Moving air. I was glad I was here in North Carolina; this prison camp, now made into a home. It had its many foolish, frivolous, and annoying rules but all I had to do was remember for a second much harder time when I was awaiting sentencing. My time in the County jail. A place where no free air like that which I was currently experiencing exists. "I'd prefer not to go back to that place again," I thought. Fortunate also to not be at a higher security Federal prison, we had a walking track with gravel. Theirs was asphalt or gravel or nonexistent. I was surely blessed even in this mess called prison. And as I placed my shoes on the tiny stones and began walking, I smiled and breathed it all in. In through my nose and out my mouth I focused on my breathing as I stepped around the quarter-mile oval track listening to my radio. Listening to one of the only two stations we could get out there.

I'm not sure how many laps I'd taken around that track in the last year, but I knew for certain it was a lot. It had become my place of peace. The place I would go when I realized I needed a bit of serenity. When I seemed to need grounding. When I came unglued: mad, sad, agitated, extremely pissed, this track had a way of medicating these emotions. Driving them back down hard like strong liquor. No longer was it drugs or alcohol I turned to; it was this track. In the form of a natural pill, one I had never bothered to explore as a free man. It's funny what you learn to do to keep yourself sane when options run low and worldly vices aren't accessible. Like writing I suppose. The story I had crammed into my footlocker. The one Gary had inspired me to write. The one Logan seemed pleading for me to finish. "If I did finish it and nothing became of it, at least I could say it freed me from this place for a while. Like this track was now releasing me." I thought as I walked.

A few focused laps now completed I began noticing the other inmates doing what I was, de-compressing. Our work and downtime schedules were pretty much the same, it was the standard affair, day in and day out. The same guys on the track like the day before, and the day before that. I saw among them a man who bunked in the same housing unit as me and was a neighboring inmate to my cell. He was one of the few whose opinion I appreciated. I appreciated him especially for the things he didn't necessarily have to say or do and didn't. In my current world of the confined, it's the things you don't say, more times than not, that make you who you are. "Be about it, don't talk about it" is the phrase most use. He was about peace and self-improvement. You could tell in his attitude and demeanor they were things he lived in and strived for more of. One of those spirits you can sense their decency. An improving soul, to say the least. As I approached him on the track, I turned my radio down. His opinion I respected, and his opinion is something I felt at that moment was something I needed. I proceeded to go into detail about what I'd experienced in my cell with the Sports Illustrated article and its coincidences. About the unread 'Forgiveness Letter' Gary had left. About my story. About the writer's block, I'd been plagued with. I told him about the story Gary had told me about loving myself. I told him I wasn't sure what was happening, but I was certain something most definitely was. A Universal calling, a sign from God, an epiphany, Logan, a Godsend. I was letting it all out. After a few contemplative laps of hearing my ramblings, Mike spoke up. What he said to me next, I would have no clue would change me forever. But I knew it changed my mind and spirit's direction right then and there. I had no idea it would be a prescription to self-love, peace, and freedom in the long run, but I knew I was hearing a prescription to something written as the Logan Effect was now rippling through Mikes' voice. The missing link in my long mental block had arrived. "Hey man, it seems you got a lot on your plate. Have you ever thought about writing a 'Forgiveness Letter' to yourself?" he offered. Mike's words sunk deep and fast into my consciousness like the Narcan. The Guardian Angel. Lifesaving. He didn't know the reason I had picked up my pace to get ahead of him. It was so he couldn't see how aghast I had become. I felt like I was getting choked up over it, but I wasn't sure. That feeling in your eyes just before you cry. Sometimes you can subdue it, sometimes you can't. "Thanks, Mike" I yelled back.

In that moment I knew what I had to do. Stepping off the track I headed back towards my cell. I had something to read I'd been ignoring. Something that wouldn't start with my family or friends. It would start with myself. I got to my cell and flung my footlocker open grabbing the 'Forgiveness Letter'. I was now searching for a way to forgive myself with an overwhelming feeling that it was something this entire road had been leading to. I hopped into my bed, cracked open the letter the Old Man had left for me, and read…

16

PERSONALIZED FORGIVENESS...

...'TO' ME.

"*Dear Cody,*

I sense your pain. I sense it is one I have felt many times before. Though yours will always be more severe to you personally than mine, nonetheless, they are both pains born out of unforgiveness. Born out of someone doing us wrong or doing someone we love wrong. Born out of someone not living up to what we expected of them. And, most all, born out of them not making right, that which they have done wrong. With that, I thought I would share with you something that happened to me not long ago.

One day out of pure frustration, I asked myself, 'Why am I not forgiving this person? I know it says somewhere that I am supposed to. I know it says somewhere that it is the best thing for me to do. But I don't. Why don't I? Why not now? Why not before now?'

Then I heard this inside my head......

'You're not really digging very hard to find out the 'why'. You're somehow comfortable in the misery of being mad and angry. You continue to be bound by the negative thoughts of it all! You're just not ready! You still see forgiving as surrendering. You still see forgiving as just not fair! Just not deserving of him! Just not right! You are

just not comfortable with him getting 'no condemnation' for what he has done to you. You suffered so why shouldn't he?'

I found myself getting worked up at this point and I could feel it. I didn't like the feeling, but it was very familiar. I'd felt it hundreds of times before, if not more. Then the voice in my head took off again...

'You don't understand this. Maybe, just maybe you don't want to understand this. You believe that you cannot personally make it right, he has to make it right. He has to adjust. He has to turn. Not you!'

This voice was now running long and getting repetitive. It seemed to be rambling over and over the same mantra it had since he first did this to me so many years ago. It was making me dizzy. Then I asked, in hopes, someone was listening...

'Where will it end? Is there really an end to these maddening thoughts and feelings?'

That someone must have heard me because the response came instantaneously...

'It ends when you start 'looking' at it differently. Until then, it will not change. Until then, it will not go away.' It continued...

'When you start looking at and accepting in faith that there is a 'bigger' plan and a 'bigger' picture for your whole life than getting caught up in this 'loop' of frustration, bitterness, and anger, then it will change for you. In a positively dramatic way, it will, because it is about God's plan and God's picture for your life, not yours. There is a Higher calling and a Higher purpose for you to be going through all this. A purpose that has nothing to do with your control or reasoning, but God's alone. You have been unwilling to yield to this, therefore, you not only don't forgive, you can't forgive! No one truly and completely forgives outside of God. It is a Spiritual

phenomenon, not a human one. All you have to do is look around you and you will find anywhere you turn confirmation of how well human forgiveness isn't working. Then again even better, just look at how well it is working for you.'

Now this voice was getting louder and clearer as if somehow my ears had just popped from the pressure of being underwater...

'No one truly and completely forgives outside of God, as even Jesus went to God. "Father, forgive them, for they know not what they do." (Lk23:34)'

'It is by God that you forgive, not by you alone.

It is you asking God to forgive him.

It is you asking God to forgive you, first.

It is you asking God to remove the pain of these transgressions.

He forgives him.

He forgives you.

He gives you Peace, beyond all understanding.

He frees you up to move on with your life, bigger and better for it.'

'The fact that we are having this conversation is living proof that it is true and that you are receptive to change and have really known all along that it wasn't possible by you alone.'

I realized just then that I was crying but they were not tears of pain but tears of a warm joyful feeling. Tears of a hopeful feeling. A feeling that this situation could change, and now would change. It was the 'would change' that got me the most. As if I had reached a point of no return. A point where I felt some peace come over me with visions of a future of less pain inside myself toward the one who had harmed me. I wondered how this could be when I had done nothing but have an internal conversation over the last few minutes. Maybe, just maybe I was already 'looking' at it differently. Maybe I was already 'thinking' about it differently. Maybe this was the actual beginning of 'processing' it differently. Could I now begin 'acting' differently?

Then it hit me, the reason for this different state of mind was the fact that for the first time I felt like I was 'not alone' in this. That 'someone' was with me. That 'someone' was going to see this through with me. That 'someone' had just lifted some weight from my shoulders. It was that 'someone' in my head, that Voice I had been conversing with and who was now with me in all of this... God. I now cried even more.

When I regained my composure, I looked up and I thought "thank you". This caused me to immediately drop my head again and say "Dear God please forgive me for my unforgiveness. Please forgive him also. Help me to begin the process of forgiving him. Please help me to find peace within this life and for him also. Give me the strength to know that you have a plan not only for me in all of this but for him. Help me to remember that I, as well as he, can only be convicted to change through you, in your way, in your season, for your reason. And that I am only capable and responsible for how and when I respond to this process of change in me and not him. He is in your hands, not mine. I am now in your hands. Thank you."

Later that day I found myself out at the prison's stone tables writing out everything I could remember of this incident from earlier in the day. As I neared what I thought was the end and came upon the part about 'processing' and 'acting' differently I stopped and began to try and think about what this should look like. And, *as you probably will guess from my telling of what happened earlier, I hear a calling as if a Voice were in my head.*

This time he said, 'You need to write a note of forgiveness to him." so I wrote a heading in my journal PROCESSING AND ACTING, and underneath it put; Draft a note of forgiveness. Instantly I heard 'I asked you to write a note, not make a note to write a note.' Wow, I guess that means I'm really supposed to actually write it now. So, I took a deep breath and wrote:

· · ·

'Dad, I want you to know that as much as I have hated you over these years, in some way I have loved you more. I am sick and tired of harboring these awful, negative feelings toward you. I am tired of trying to figure out an answer to why you would possibly have treated me the way you did. Why you would have been so seemingly mean in your actions and your words toward me over the years. I had hoped that you would sense the pain that you had caused me and out of love for me come forward and accepted it, apologized for it, and helped me heal from it. This had never happened which in itself seemed to continually add to my pain. But something amazing has happened to me today that I want to share with you and then give you something. Today, as I once again was muddling over my pain and woes seemingly at your hands, God came to me in my thoughts and forgave me. Yes, he forgave me for all the awful, hurtful, vindictive, and vengeful thoughts I have had toward you over this. He actually forgave me when I thought if anyone needed his forgiveness it was you, not me! But I realized then and there that He was right. That no matter what you had done and why you had done it to me it was wrong for me to react in such a way. So, he forgave me, even though I had done nothing to be worthy of such forgiveness. As soon as that happened something incredible came over me. I no longer wanted to be mad at you. I no longer wanted to be 'pissed off' at you. I no longer wanted to be frustrated with you. I was tired of it. And just like that its appeal was gone. Yes, really gone. Therefore, I want you to know that from this moment forward I forgive you, period, I hold nothing against you for any of your past words or actions toward me. And I pray that you may find peace within all of this yourself. This is now between you and God and no longer me. You are free from my wrath. I harbor it no more. I give it to you freely, as it was given to me. I love you. Gary'

. . .

Cody, I assure you that I will never forget that day. I have gone back to it, and also my notes many times when 'unforgiveness' has raised its ugly head again in my life. And every time I have ended with another 'note of forgiveness' to that person or persons. And the same release has come over me without fail. Does that mean I never have a negative thought about the past and its happenings? Heck no. It does still happen from time to time as the 'dark side' is always ready to pull me back in. The difference is that first, the negative painful thought lasts literally a microsecond, ok sometimes a few minutes. This is because my thoughts now go to 'I wonder how God is working 'good' in their life today?' and 'I hope they have found peace in Him for their life.' And secondly, I realize that no matter where they are in the process, it is a part of the big picture of life for them and me, that I know as I live and breathe it is still unfolding, for the good.

Now, Dad was long gone when I wrote out that note to him, but the release was just as real in that all that I had harbored for so long was gone. Just like that, gone. And it stays gone and I look back and now see the many joys and gifts Dad did, and left for me. My focus is not on what he didn't do, or say, but the goodness of his life. Of course, I had to test to see if this spiritual phenomenon of forgiveness would actually work on a live person. One that not only I harbored pain from but one that continued to pile it on by their actions, or lack of actions. So, I took the next most painful person after my father, my once close brother of 57 years. After I plead guilty and was sentenced to Federal Prison, he broke off relations with me. Not only disowning me as a brother but notifying the Prosecutor that I had contacted him without his authorization. That prompted a cease and desist order of 'no further contact' not only with him but 'all' my family members. Also, including his children and the other nieces and nephews with who I had a very close relationship. So, this was a pretty painful one, to say the least.

I went back out to the table with my journal and notepad. Then, I said a prayer asking God to forgive me for all the things I harbored against him, thinking on all of them specifically. (this was difficult stuff) Then, as before, I wrote out a detailed 'note of forgiveness' to him very similar to the one I had written to our Dad. As I was emotionally writing I could literally feel a weight like before being slowly lifted. Once completed, I read it in its entirety out loud and experienced emotional freedom. I knew it was literally done. It was over. I could feel no more pain but actual joy that it had taken on this new light. It was now between him and God. What he did with it was not for me to decide. I prayed, and still pray, to this day that the Holy Spirit continues to soften his heart and loosen the strongholds in his mind so that he can find Peace. The same Peace that I have found, that I was given.

Cody, I hope and pray also that this letter will help you process what you are going through so that you can experience it too. It will unlock you, from your very self, when it happens. And you will know whose hand was in it... Gods.'
Peace, Gary Martel

'p.s. I have highlighted the steps to forgiveness that I was asked to take, and continue to take in my life. This is as close as I can get to what they sounded like when I heard them.

1. *Ask God to forgive you personally for 'all' you have harbored toward this person and in the situation.*

2. *Ask God to forgive them for 'all' they have harbored toward you and in the situation.*

3. *Write out a 'note of forgiveness' stating that you have been forgiven by God and now you are forgiving them completely and will be praying for their peace going forward.*

4. *Now, forgive them by reading the note out loud allowing your emotions to be released and restored.*

5. *Say a Prayer of Healing, Goodness, and Peace into their life. (A blessing like in 1 Peter 3:4)*

6. *Thank God for the gift of this forgiveness.*

7. *Receive your 'forgiveness'* as it is now complete.*

This forgiveness is not predicated on you sending them the note, reading it to them, and/or them accepting it! This is about your freedom from unforgiveness. Their ultimate freedom from unforgiveness must come from God and their personal actions in acceptance of it or not. Just keep praying Healing, Goodness, and Peace into their life, even if they continue to 'ratchet up the rhetoric' within their yet unforgiving life. Then you keep moving forward in your life, being thankful every day for your newfound, and continual growing Peace'

. . .

...'FROM' ME.

I put the letter down and stared forward at the white brick in my cell. A room free from stimuli. The institution I occupied, a colorless cage. Drab at best. My vision usually searching for some resemblance of color in here. Now, however, my eyes fixed forward in a trance. Unblinking, I couldn't see past what I'd just read. 'The Forgiveness Letter', a blueprint to uncovering a life of peace. Or so he had said. Yet, I doubted its effectiveness on myself. "Could it work?" I whispered. He had waited to give me this until he left. I was pissed. I had questions. A solution all this time, crumpled in my footlocker. I was seething to get to the 'new starting line'. "You knew this is what I needed though, didn't you?" A question I asked the old man that wasn't there. He knew that this too was part of the story. The journey of discovery.

I grabbed my notebook and pen. Still holding 'The Forgiveness Letter', I placed it on my desk as a guide. I knew right then and there that for me to move forward I needed to write a letter of forgiveness. Yet not beginning with others but, to myself. The old man had not mentioned that, but it didn't matter, the Voice telling me to do it was not his. It seemed to be brought to light by the magazine article about Logan and solidified as the right thing to do by the talk with Mike on the track. I touched the black ink pen to the paper and scribbled two words. Two words that, seemingly the start of a normal letter, were anything but. My world pouring from the pen tip, a stop in the levy come undone. Flowing over me, the rush of emotions too great for my shoulders to burden. As I wrote "Dear Cody" I had no clue the power of the letter would be that great, the power of forgiveness. Two words are all I got before I started to cry.

I felt a presence behind me and turned from my desk. Shocked to see myself standing behind me, I couldn't believe what I was seeing. A Cody I recognized but remembered hating. A man covered in tattoos, the evil radiating from his body. He looked high too. Demented to say the least. It was the Cody that had lived in me all along, a parasite. The "Dear Cody" had forced him out, eradicated his hold from the host that was me. Now, I could see him in his ugliness, the nasty addicted human he was. I stared at the Cody staring back at me, was afraid of what I saw. A monster. Fearful and unkind he had been born out of unforgiveness. Of course, the letter was proving that. I put the pen back to the paper and began to write again.

"Dear Cody, I want you to know that as much as I have hated you over these years, in some ways I have loved you more. I am sick and tired of harboring these awful, negative feelings towards you. I am tired of trying...."

I stopped writing. Put the pen down and realized I had simply been copying Gary's letter. It was what I need to say but not how 'I' needed to say it. Crumpling the first, I started over.

• • •

"Dear Cody, I'm sorry for putting you in this place, you shouldn't be here."

Tears again coming to my eyes confirmed that what I was writing was sinking in. To my soul. To Cody, I was reading the letter as I wrote it. I felt a burden lifting. Not a lot, but enough to feel its weight lessen. I was surprised myself to realize I had only gotten a sentence out and I could already feel the power of the letter. I continued.

"You're an amazing person with a ton of potential Cody. I know this place isn't where you want to be, but you know it's what you needed. To forgive yourself. To face yourself, clean and drug-free. You were caught in a terrible addiction and I'm so glad you're alive. We have an amazing life ahead of us. God, I am sorry for the person I was and can still be at times. All I care about is this point forward, not the past. The New Starting Line.

"The new starting line," I thought as I stopped writing. I quickly returned, pushing on knowing this is where Gary had been encouraging me to get to.

"I don't care about your voids anymore Cody. They are in the past. From this point forward you will be void-free. You will fill your voids with the love from God, not drugs or alcohol. Cody, you're important to a lot of people. Your family and friends, they

love you immensely. When you get done with this letter, you're going
to write a forgiveness letter to all of them. You're going to forgive
them, and they are going to forgive you. This will happen because
God will forgive you. You are the rose that is just as beautiful as
a seed as you are a flower. You're a ten Cody, in Gods' eyes, you've
always been a ten."

I stopped the letter and looked through glassy eyes at the Cody I had
eradicated. He was holding his head in his hands, weeping uncontrollably. He was now young though, and much smaller. No skull
tattoos covering his body. The Cody of the younger days. Before the
Fentanyl and steroids, he looked much healthier. As I sat there looking at my younger self, I couldn't help but cry even more knowing
the hardship he'd endure later in life. "If only I could turn back time
and stop him," I thought. But as I looked up at my younger self
thinking these thoughts, I heard God. In my cell writing a forgiveness letter to myself, I heard God's Voice. "You must go through
this so others may be saved. So, others can discover the power of
forgiving." In that moment as God's words sunk into my head, I
couldn't help but think about Logan. Finally, I understood why I
had been chosen to read the Sports Illustrated article. "You must
experience this loss so thousands of others can live." I heard myself
say. 'The Logan Effect' had come full circle. I put my head on the
letter I was writing to myself and wept. My tears blotting the ink. I
could feel Logan and his teammate's presence in my cell. The ones
who had inspired me to keep writing. The loss they'd experienced
so thousands could live and to not let another single second go by
without doing what I'd finally discovered; a true cure to free myself
from the darkness I'd harbored. The addiction. I continued writing.

"You're not an addict or a loser, weak or unworthy. Cody, you're the opposite of those things. You're strong and vibrant. Life radiates from you and you don't need drugs or alcohol to validate that. YOU see that. The only person you need to follow is God, his validation is the only validation you need. Cody, I forgive you forever. Stop thinking otherwise. Stop chasing this validation from others. You're free of that and I forgive you."

. . .

I looked up from my notepad. The droplets of tears smudged on the page. A child now in front of me. His sun-stained hair, blonde in the lights of my cell. His knees scrapped up. It was me as a child. I looked so innocent, oblivious to the place I stood. "So carefree," I thought. I remembered back to the times I was that child. I knew that's when it all began. "I miss my dad," a whisper came from him. That's all it was. "I simply miss my dad," I put the pen down. The 'Forgiveness Letter' to myself now verbal. I didn't need a pen and paper. I looked at the young boy in my cell and spoke to him like the child I was.

"Cody, you're going to go through some things in life that aren't your fault, so don't blame yourself. Love yourself and know that God will always love you back. Say your prayers before bed and always smile kid. You're perfect the way you are, don't change for anyone. I love you, buddy."

When I blinked the boy was gone. More importantly, so was the Cody I had needed to forgive. Knowing he was now gone, I got up from my desk and reach into my footlocker to grab the story I had stopped writing. A new race had just begun and an old one had just ended. I put the pen to the paper and took off, I took off from the 'new starting line'.

17

THE NEW ANTIDOTE...

...RECOGNITION

The first thing I noticed as I stepped onto the walking track wasn't the sun beaming down or the temperature outside. It was the sound of music. Not the initial wave of radiance I usually sought refuge in. The Tupac music blasting from someone's headphones had diverted my attention from the usual affair nature provided within these confines. It was a song I was familiar with. One I had listened to many times myself. The lyrics once memorized, "Hail Mary, Come with me." At least I could still remember the words of the chorus. As I lipped the song I smiled. A flood of memories returning. I briefly returned to a day, long ago when I wasn't afraid of coming to the place I now occupied. Prison. As the lyrics continued blasting from the young man's headphones, I fell in behind him on the track. After the music, the second thing I noticed was his tattoos. He had a skull collage on his arm. One similar to the design I had concocted and had almost inked. Once again, the memories flooded over me. The tattoo shops. All the hours spent sitting with a needle going in and out of my skin. I could almost feel it. The similarities eerily matched, him and I. As I walked behind him, I couldn't help but think of the younger me, who'd entered prison a few years earlier.

"He must be new here, " I wondered "I hadn't seen him before." It was hard keeping track of all the other inmates who came and went. Except of course the few I had managed to befriend. The ones that had pointed me in the direction of forgiveness. As I continued walking behind the young man, I couldn't help but wonder if this inmate would be one that I'd relate with as I had Gary and Mike. One was now gone and the other soon to be.

The Tupac music and tattoos were already a good indication of our likeness. You didn't find many guys in here you could really relate to. As the negative voice in my head attempted to convince me to keep walking and ignore this 20-something-year-old man, I knew I should probably do the opposite. I sped up next to him.

I tapped him on the shoulder, something I immediately regretted doing. Despite my time incarcerated I sometimes forgot the rules. Boundaries must be respected at all times. He quickly jerked toward me and pulled his headphones off. "Sorry about that man," I quickly said. He turned to face me with a look that didn't resemble one from the conversational type. His pace not slowing the least. He didn't respond. The removal of the headphones enough of a non-verbal cue for me to go ahead and say what I needed to. I was bugging him. "I'm Cody. I've kind of lived all over the Midwest. Iowa, Nebraska, Missouri. Where you from?" Name. Location. The standard combo of questions inmates ask to break the ice. "Tanner, from Illinois," he replied. "Nice to meet you," I said. I put my hand out and offered my peace. A compromised crossing of boundaries on both terms. He slowly put his hand out. I knew the uneasiness he felt. It had once been me. We stopped on the track and stood toe to toe. He was the same height as me, 6 foot 3. I couldn't believe how much we looked alike. As he faced me, I couldn't help but scan the skull tattoos covering his chest. "This is me," I thought. As he grabbed my hand, I immediately recognized the person behind the grip. I allowed him to do his intimidation thing. The "I'm tougher than you because I have a stronger grip thing." A move I almost expected in this place. The 'tough guy' persona was in no shortage here. As I looked into his eyes though I read a much different individual. The handshake, simply a mask. "Mind if I walk with you for a minute?" I asked. He shrugged his broad shoulders, pausing them for a second at the top. "Be my guest," he replied.

We turned back around and continued walking. His headphones resting around his neck. Tupac was done rapping and his playlist was now on to something different. "So, you like Tupac?" I asked. He grabbed one side of the headphones. "Oh, this. Yeah, He's not bad," he replied. I knew that wasn't what he meant so I pushed for a better answer. "C'mon man, nobody that listens to Tupac thinks he's 'not bad'. Either you love the guy, or you don't," I said. He gave a half-smile and chuckled. "Yeah, he's pretty much the greatest rapper of all time." he surmised. "I used to listen to him a lot myself. Definitely one of the best." I agreed. We had found common ground. Something I knew wouldn't be difficult. All the similarities were pretty obvious. But then again, lots of guys in here had tattoos and listened to rap music. Actually, most of them did. This guy seemed different though. I couldn't believe how much of myself I saw in him so instantly. Maybe it was the stature. Maybe it was the other features. His hair cut perhaps. Or maybe it was what he transmitted that I felt. Energy from him to me. A pain? A sadness? A void?

"So, I'm guessing you got in today?" I asked. "Yeah man, came in this afternoon," he replied. "You need anything?" I asked. I had a small number of clothes and toiletries I kept in my locker for occasions like this. There seemed nothing worse for a new guy than getting to prison and not having the bare minimum of things. If it were like my experience and he came in from another prison, he wouldn't be getting his property until at a minimum the following week. If he were a first-time prisoner, he would get less in toiletries than you get to take from a hotel bathroom. The Federal Prison issued a bright green shirt that screamed 'new guy' to anyone new to that facility no matter as a new or transferred prisoner. If you're trying to lay low and not be recognized, the Fed's make it almost impossible. I sensed that the response that came from him would be a half-truth at best. Half true like the Tupac lyrics had been. I was prepared. "Um, I pretty much got everything man. Thanks," he replied. I smiled. Our pace brisk. The sun beaming down, a slight breeze on our faces. As we continued walking, I looked over at Tanner and he looked over at me. For a brief moment, eye contact was made. "Look, man, we're not going to continue this soft-peddle exchange thing. I've been here a few years; you can ask anyone about me. This isn't some sort of angle I'm working. Saying you 'Pretty much' have everything and 'having' everything are two different things. What do you need man?" I asked. I stopped him before he could get a word out. "You know what Tanner. After this walk why don't you swing by my cell? I'll give you some of my extra stuff." I spoke. "You don't' need to thank me either. From one Midwest guy to another." Just pass it on to another new inmate who may need it one day." I continued. "Well, I appreciate it, Cody," he replied. "Not a problem," I said as we continued walking. At the time unaware that I'd soon be helping him with much, much more.

We continued to make small talk. We both seemed to realize it wasn't just the music and tattoos linking us; Tanner and I had much more in common. The similarities continued rising to the surface. The sports. The girls. College football. Tanner had played ball at the University of Illinois until a career-ending knee injury brought his NFL dreams to a screeching halt. "What'd you do after that?" I asked. Tanner looked away. His eyes scanning the long expanse of North Carolina pine trees. I had remembered first getting here and being in awe of the same thing. Hundred-foot pine trees weren't that common in the Plains states like they were here. A sight Tanner wasn't used to either. "I don't know man. One thing kind of led to the other and here I am," he replied. It wasn't what Tanner said that struck me. I understood those words with clarity beyond his understanding. It was how he said it. I knew in that young man's voice there lay a fear. A doubt. A burning passion to rid himself of a darkness that was attempting to control him. The one that had controlled him to the point of having this be his new home. "Let me guess, opiates huh?" I asked. A question with a word interjected so impacting to a man that knew its crippling power as much as I did. Its life-altering capacity. I wasn't sure how long Tanner had been clean, but I could sense in his body language the word had hit him like a ton of bricks. He stopped on the track and turned toward me saying rapidly, "I had the world in my hands, everything I could ask for, but I was living a lie. Nothing at all was fine. The pills.... they.... they made something inside me better. Then they ruined my life!" I could see the tears welling in his eyes. A glassy haze I could recognize. I ushered him casually to a bench near the track and we sat down. We both gazed forward. Words unspoken for some time. There was no need to talk. We could feel each other's words. We could hear each other loud and clear despite us saying nothing. We watched as the other inmates shuffled around the track. "Yeah man," he said. "They ruined my life," he continued. I looked over at him. I thought to myself that Gary had probably recognized the same pain in me. I said what I thought to be the most appropriate thing I could. "You know Tanner, there's a way to not make you feel like that anymore." A statement. Not a question but a statement. He turned and looked at me. The large pine trees waving behind us. "What do you mean?" he asked.

...INJECTION

"You know Tanner, I was you. I was exactly like you. We haven't been through the same things, but I promise you we've both experienced the same void. The loss. The fear. The voice that's probably talking to you in your head right now. When I got here and the dust finally settled, I set out on a quest to rid myself of the pain I felt," I said. Tanner was the first person since I'd put some finality to my manuscript that I was about to openly discuss any of my revelations with. I felt as uneasy about discussing my discovery as I'm sure he was hearing it. He looked at me with a quizzical expression. I switched gears. "When did you start working out and playing sports? You're a big kid, must have been early," I said. He smiled. "Yeah, my entire life. I probably started lifting at 12 and never looked back," he said. His answer was one I expected. "And it got you the attention you weren't getting at home, didn't it?" I asked as if to challenge him. I saw immediately that he knew I was right. Yet, he didn't really want to admit it. The fumbling with his headphones and the shrugging of his shoulders, a sure sign I was tapping into the pain of his void as if salt on a wound. "Yeah, mom was pretty busy. Dad lived in another state," he said. Looking down at his feet and now fumbling with his headphone wires, I could see the words resonating. "Let me guess. You'd never touched drugs until sports ended. Then it was almost like you put as much passion into taking pills as you had playing ball," I said. Clearly, I hit a nerve. He shot up from the bench, threw his headphones on, and started walking around the track. I followed suit. I lagged behind, waiting for him to calm down. I wasn't a professional with this stuff and realized I had said too much. "Leave me alone," he yelled over his shoulder. I stopped. Paused for a second and turned around back towards the bench. I had no idea what to do. I recognized that I wasn't equipped for this kind of conversation, or so the negative voice told me. "This kind of healing isn't for you," the voice said. I sat back down and started praying, "God, please help me say the right things to this kid. You helped me write this story and discover myself, now please help me to help others do the same." As other inmates passed me, their faces slightly skewed at the sight of me praying to myself. I didn't care. I put my head down and continued praying to God. Begging for help with Tanner. It had only been a couple of minutes when I looked up again. Tanner was there. He had come back. "Thank you, God," I thought to myself. I knew he had been crying and I knew he didn't want me to look at him, so I didn't. Tanner began to speak. "This voice you talk about, it talks to me too. It's telling me to get high and worse. It hurts fighting it all the time. I can't believe I ended up in prison man. I can't believe I let everyone down. I can't believe I let myself down," he said now putting his head in his hands as he took a seat beside me. Tanner sobbed. He said it. The last sentence, a Universal explosion, sending me wide-eyed for an instant. He was blaming himself just like I had. I gave him a couple of big pats on the back and told him it wasn't his fault. "Don't beat yourself up," I said. "You can't blame yourself," I continued. I didn't know what to say next, so I sat there, continued looking forward as Tanner regained composure. Across the prison yard, I saw some inmates working in the garden surrounding one of the buildings. They were tending to the rose bush plants on the compound. Then, it hit me. "Thank you, God," I said to myself.

I began to tell Tanner the story of the rose. Not as good as Gary had done albeit decent enough to get my point across. "You see Tanner, despite your current situation you're still a 'ten'. You've always been a 'ten' man," I said. At that point, I realized I needed to humble myself and open up to Tanner. Let him know about 'my' story. So, I did, in abbreviated form, without losing the important pieces. I started from the beginning and told him all the details that led to my incarceration. I stopped when I got to the part about Gary leaving. About him giving me the forgiveness letter. The struggle with finishing my story and finding the Sports Illustrated article. The part about talking with Mike on this very track. About forgiving myself. I had stopped just before revealing the part Tanner needed to discover himself. "So, then what happened?" Tanner asked. "What happened for you to close the void?" he continued. "The drugs, the women, the steroids and self-worth. How can you just sit here and say you'll never do it again?" he asked excitedly. I got up. Didn't answer his questions. Just started walking back towards the housing units. "Where are you going?" Tanner yelled. "You didn't answer my question," he continued. "Let's go get that stuff from my locker," I yelled back. Tanner got up from the bench and followed me off the track into the housing unit. Sure, we were going to get clothes and toiletries. But unbeknownst to him, we were going to get him to begin the search for the antidote, to begin the journey of his healing process. We were going to get him my rough typed manuscript. He followed.

"Along with this bag full of stuff I want you to take this," I said holding my only full copy in my hand. He grabbed it from me and held it like it was a rabid animal of some kind. Arm's length and face back in case it might just lash out. He wasn't exactly sure what he was holding. I was though. He was holding the path to the cure of forgiving himself. He was holding the potential power of forgiveness. "Well, thanks for the stuff man," he said, throwing the bound manuscript into the bag. Tanner left my cell unaware of what he possessed if used to its fullest potential. I smiled. I knew it wouldn't be long before Tanner would be wanting to talk again.

...LIBERATION!

Days later I was walking around the track when I felt a tap on my shoulder. I had my headphones in, slightly tranced, and lost in my music. I turned to see a vivacious Tanner with an expression I could only recognize as being as if 'born-again'. One I'd seen myself display. "He read the makings of my book," I thought to myself as I pulled down the headphones. 'What's up?" I spoke. "Hey man, you mind if I catch a few laps with you, it's about your story?" he said. His demeanor resembling anything but that of an incarcerated individual. He was full of a life I hadn't seen in a lot of people in here. I smiled as I recognized what was happening. What 'had' happened. As we walked Tanner went into great detail about the chapters that impacted him. "So, the forgiveness letter Gary left you. What a life-changing letter." his voice erratic. "And... the discovery of your own forgiveness. Your letter to yourself. I mean. Can you believe it's as easy as recognizing your importance and letting all your burdens go by writing forgiveness letters to yourself and all those you hold animosity toward?" he said through short-filled gasps. I said the only thing I could really think to say at that moment, "God is wonderful isn't he Tanner, as in doing it for us He showed us the way?" Tanner reached into his back pocket and pulled a folded piece of paper out. It appeared as though it had been folded and refolded quite a few times. Recognizing what it was I once again motioned for him to sit down just like I had a couple of days prior. We stepped off the track to the exact same bench with those same big pine trees rising behind it. He held the letter in his big hands. I could tell by the slight ripples of the moving paper he was nervous. I waited for him to speak. I knew this was an important moment in his life. Possibly the most important to date. I waited patiently while he mustered enough courage to speak. "I want to read this to you," he said. He unfolded the paper and stared at the black ink scribbled across the page. "Tanner, you know you don't have to do that. The letter isn't meant to be read to anyone. It's for you, nobody else," I said. "I know, but I want to read it to you," he said again. He had made up his mind. I sat there as Tanner cleared his throat. I had been here. I had done the same thing in my cell. I had expunged the monster that had consumed me, and I began filling the void. It was a moment in time I remembered like I'm sure Tanner would too. For a moment time stopped for me. The book. The discovery. The true purpose of it all had cumulated to this very point in time. Helping others discover forgiveness. True forgiveness. Tanner began to speak. Two words. Two words were all he got out before he crumbled onto the track and we began praying together. "Dear Tanner".

EPILOGUE

A "Perfect Storm" is defined as: a particularly bad or critical state of affairs, arising from a number of negative and unpredictable factors.

A LASTING NARCAN

The revelation of my life in the 'Perfect Storm of Addiction' and my release from that storm by recognizing and embracing the antidote for addiction, 'forgiveness' has now been put to paper. Believe me when I tell you it was the hardest thing I've ever done, and I'd like to think I had done some pretty hard things when I was in that storm. The looming questions even for myself in rereading it begs this position. I can't convince you, nor will I ever try to convince you that I don't hear negative voices anymore. Eliminating them wasn't my intention when I set out on this journey. I knew that to be an impossible task. It was to find what it would take, or who it would take to gain power and control over them. I also never set out to be 'healed' or 'cured' to the extent that I'd never again be called to apply what I learned in writing this book. Applying anew 'forgiveness' and feeling the 'power' of it take control.

Although the negative voices still exist, I believe them to have no real power over my life anymore. It was incredibly liberating to discover my true worth, because the darkness that had aimed to consume me, was crippling me. By finally understanding and accepting my importance first to God and then to myself, I've been able to fill my painful voids with love. So, it doesn't really matter what the negative voices try to convince me of now, they're called out as gibberish and relegated back to the low place from which they came.

Let me reiterate. When I discovered my true worth and was able to accept the forgiveness of myself from God, life began again for me. I was able to move forward and begin to forgive others who had seemingly been a part of creating those painful voids. I've read book after book after book trying to discover the secret to happiness, searching endlessly for it. I never would have guessed all the answers would be found not in the searching through other stories but in the writing of 'this' story, my story. It became a personal journey of discovery within my life. What was revealed allowed the answers to my many questions to be heard clearly. The real story isn't the 'book' itself. The real story occurred in the discovery, those revelations that you have now witnessed me expose. The journey in the writing.

Let me say what is most important. **The biggest story for you is not my story. It is what YOU have been discovering about yourself while reading it.** You recognize that the answers I searched for did not come easy. You now realize they will not come easy for you either. Yet, in traveling the journey through my life, hopefully, you now know they will come for you too, and from Whom they will come. Conquering the obstacles that hold us back never is easy, especially when we go it alone. Relationships, self-worth, and addictions were a few of my obstacles. In learning the importance of, and the how-to of 'forgiveness' made these obstacles no longer a burden.

You have been able to witness that although I am incarcerated between these walls, I gained freedom from the worst kind of imprisonment. Freedom from the 'perfect storm' of a self-destructive life. That is what embracing the revelations that were exposed during the writing of my life did for me. And it will for you too, as you delve into the journey of your own life.

In truth, the real reason I found myself incarcerated was because I didn't love myself. I thought I did but clearly, I was confused as I was doing some horrible things to someone I believed I loved, myself. The overdoses were just one example of that. The cure to the reckless life I was living wasn't a pill for 'depression' or for a doctor to diagnose me with some sort of mental condition. They frequently did just that and I kind of hoped it was so as it might have been easier for me. Yet the solution to my problems came to me in the form of a different prescription, a different diagnosis. In the form of a 'Forgiveness Letter'. By studying it and learning the 'why to' and the 'how to' of forgiveness, all the puzzle pieces to my happiness began to fit together. In 'forgiveness' I found a way to free myself from my past and all the negativity I'd harbored towards myself and others. Many doctors and many books had solutions 'they' believed would rid me of 'my 'pain and 'my 'suffering. All meant to 'cure' me. Yet, as hard as I tried to embrace them, none seemed to work. Only when I discovered the directions in the 'Forgiveness Letter', to 'forgive myself' did I make any true progress. Now that it has been embraced and activated, I am coming back together. Yes, together slowly but together, nonetheless. It has not been easy, and it has taken quite some work. However, it has been much, much easier than filling the voids of pain in the way I had been filling them with my previous activities, drugs, and alcohol.

Through this entire process, I've had to learn how to subdue the doubt that tries to creep in. It came in many forms. With the seemingly continuous writing that I did in my cell or the typing of it out on the central computer, I became a visible target for its attack. I was ridiculed by many inmates. I would often hear "Why are you writing so much?", "What do you think you're doing, writing a book?", "Who do you think is going to read something from a prisoner like you?" The comments were endless and the doubt they were designed to create were constantly at my mental door, which makes my next point so important. Like the voices of doubt, I'm also learning to gain control over the voices of fear in my life. The 'Old Man' that helped me discover forgiveness also constantly pushed me to write. To get my story on paper. If it weren't for his positive encouragement, in the beginning, this story probably wouldn't have been completed. The journey might have been abandoned because before I discovered my self-worth the doubt and fear that haunted me was great and powerful. It was hard for me to step out of my comfort zone of the routines of my life that supported me. Believe me, in pushing to write 'honestly' of my life most definitely took me out of my comfort zone. When I was internally scared of the possibility that every decision I made might fail, life got pretty stagnant inside. You probably know exactly what I am speaking of. I remained caught in my comfort zone. In a growth-less place. Yet, growth was the very thing I was hoping to obtain. But, for me to do so I had to find a way to jump through the hoop of fear in order to get to the area just outside my comfort zone, where I might have a chance to begin again. It became apparent that this was unavoidable if I had any chance of genuine growth. You may be coming to the same realization. I was terrified to write this book. The voices said,

"Would people even want to read it?" "Can I even write in the first place?", "Does where I am writing from discrediting its truth?"

The voice. The doubt. The fear. You know now that you can trust me when I tell you that I understand their debilitating power. **In writing this book I hoped to make it possible for each and every reader to see how I was able to overcome my doubt and fear. How to gain power and control over that negative voice that spoke of them in my ear and in my mind.** Grabbing ahold of my own 'will power' and saying, "screw it" and jumping through the hoop was certainly a big part of it. But I discovered that a bigger part in conquering the lies of doubt and fear was through the discovery of, and the decision in 'forgiveness'. Yet, the biggest of all was my discovery that I was truly not alone. That I didn't have to rely solely on my own 'will power' in the process of change. That there was a power greater than mine that was available to me in my new journey. The Power of the One who had first 'forgiven me'. The One who allowed me to see myself as forgiven. The One that then empowered me, through Him to go on and truly, genuinely, and completely 'forgive' others, 'God'.

While embracing this truth, I have found that together as I continue to clean my life's slate of those many burdens, through 'forgiveness', the doubt and fear of failure in them is being conquered. I chose to for the first time in a long time humble myself to understand it's all part of the process of my growth. I am now able to accept 'failing' for what it is, one of the ultimate forms of my growth. I don't have to go looking for it or create it on my own. It's a funny thing that it finds me as it finds you. The most successful people on the planet understand this concept. Failure is a beautiful thing based upon how we view it and how we use it. When we return from our failures, we are more resilient, more knowledgeable, more understanding, and more capable to take the next steps of our life journey.

Our society, even down to some of our loving families, have made failure such a vicious word when in reality it's something we should embrace. They are as confused as you and I once were. Failing happens. It's a reality in life. Should we let failure dictate our every decision? Absolutely not. We should turn failure around by deciding to dictate from our new position of Power what the failure means for our growth.

I embarked on this journey originally worrying if it would 'fail' or 'succeed'. I knew that the statistics for a successful book was not on my side as a first-time author, let alone a prisoner. Up until the point when I discovered the Power of Forgiveness negative statistics like that consumed me. The fear of failing was great. After discovering forgiveness, those negative thoughts no longer reverberated through my mind. Eventually, I began to tell myself that the book's success based on sales was an inaccurate indicator of its success. My mind went to success being defined by "If only one person who reads my book is able to discover what I discovered and go on to have a fulfilling joyful life free of addiction, then the book would be a 100% success!" That realization moved me to continue to write it. I have leaned heavily at times on His Power in me to push through the voice of my fears and doubts. In that state, I came to recognize that the book's true worth and success had already worked miracles in my life. I was becoming quite glad that I continued to write it. My family and friends became living testimonies to it and would tell you so. Those relationships that at one time simply existed now thrive better than ever. I used to turn chapters into my Editor with a grocery list of self-doubt statements. "I'm not sure where I was going here." "Good luck editing this chapter, it's horrible," I'd say. "Why are we doing this, nobody wants to hear my story?" Now, however, I write this very sentence with a smile on my face, knowing everything will be just fine. Believe me when I say I work diligently taking this attitude and wisdom into all my new ventures.

I knew I was beating the voice by getting one step ahead of it. I could almost predict what lie it was about to put into my head before it even came. I was empowered in facing my fears and doubts. I was mending relationships by extending the releasing Power of forgiveness to them. Could it get any better from behind a prison fence? Well, let me tell you it did. My newfound self-worth has been improving my overall well-being too. Those devilish tattoos are still reminders of what can happen when self-pity, doubt, fear, and overall the voice of negativity internally consumed me. I came to know that my outer image, still marked from the past, is not an indication of what's going on inside me anymore. I genuinely feel amazing! I did a number on my body with all the drugs I had consumed. You might well know the reality of that. When I became incarcerated, I was on a handful of prescription medications to keep my mind in check, now I take none. I now find myself saying "Why do I need pills as the 'go to' solution? I have something much more powerful than medication to go to first. My mind is now kept in check with a prescription called 'forgiveness'. When I remind myself that I am forgiven and that I have forgiven others I no longer harbor the stress that beforehand was so debilitating. You know that debilitating stress as well. It's poison to our bodies. The high blood pressure, the anxiety, the depression, the headaches. The list goes on and on.

All these physical conditions caused by harboring stress from un-forgiveness. The stress from when we do not accept ourselves for who we are, an amazing '10', as God sees us.

My hope is that you find yourself here, ready to encounter the free-dom that I did. In seeking this new way, this new antidote, the chains of pain will be broken. At whatever point in your path to self-love and forgiveness you currently find yourself, freedom is never as far away as the negative voice will have you believe it to be. God believes in you as a '10' and He believes in your life potential as a '10'. What you're reading right now at this very moment is proof of that Power and Discovery coming alive in you. How do I know? If it weren't true, you would have put the book down long ago! But you didn't. Accept that there is great meaning in this fact. Keep the search for more going. I believe in you, because I was you.

First using the power that comes to you when you recognize your new position as a '10' makes it possible for you to 'will' changes for your life into existence. Mastering it to create your future has endless possibilities. Believe me, it can be done. I wanted to put it to the test by activating it with some of my family and friends. In my quest, I was first 'compelled' to ask my Mom to come to see me, instead of continuing to wait painfully for her to find the perfect time. I knew the power of what I was using was immense but only when I actually heard my name over the prison's loudspeaker, "Cody Lanus report to visitation," did I truly understand its capacity to begin moving events.

When I saw my Mom and brother standing in the visiting room, I couldn't hold back the tears. I didn't care if I was surrounded by other inmates either. "How did this happen? What part did I play in 'willing' this visit into existence? It seemed a small task to ask my Mom to come yet, I could never before bring myself to have 'the' conversation with her. The voice that spoke in my head before I arrived on this journey of the rose just wouldn't allow it. My pride and feeling of little self-worth in her eyes kept me blind. The doubt and fear within it previously consumed me. "Your Mom's too busy." "She doesn't' have the time in her schedule to come see you." "She's got better things to do than come to prison and waste her day." After remembering my position within 'The Rose' story I reframed what the voice was telling me, and I got on the phone and asked her to come to see me? What's even more powerful is that the One who saw me as a '10' was working in my mom at the same time. Lo and behold, she had recently been thinking about visiting me herself and had her hotel rooms already booked before I even called!

I found that when you begin by recognizing and applying your position within 'The Rose' story into your life, an entire host of positive energy begins to flood your way. The universe itself seems to begin making way to your commands. All God wants is for you to begin to see what He does so clearly, your position in His eyes. Then the path and potential for forgiveness to become the next step opens up for you.

It is a process, and it is one that as you commit to it will see you through the steps that lay ahead. Even with my first success in having my mom coming to see me, that small negative voice worked to creep back in. "Surely that first visit was a coincidence, right? It wasn't something bigger than that, was it? It wasn't orchestrated by something or someone bigger than me, right?", it began speaking. In quieting that voice and taking action once again I proved it was in fact wrong. A few weeks later I reached out as I had to my mom, with one of my best friends Kreed, and asked for a visit. Once again, this visit came about by overcoming that small negative voice by remembering my position in God's eyes and taking action. Kreed had been with me through everything. Through my highs and lows, my addiction, the sentencing. He remained a loyal friend through my entire incarceration. Once again instead of allowing the voice of negativity to consume me I faced down the voice and asked Kreed to drive across the country and see me. The next week we were sitting across from each other in visitation! I couldn't believe it. "Ask him to visit, I'm sure he'd love to come." "Tell him you miss him." These actions that got him to visit were once quite difficult for me, and still are uncomfortable at times yet, these positive thoughts were becoming easier and easier to verbalize. I'd never been one to tell those how I truly felt but now that I was telling them, my life was changing for the better. They simply needed verbalization and I needed to jump accompanied by the better voice, through the hoop of fear to grow. By controlling and reordering the voice of the 'fear of rejection' and 'low internal self-worth', I was able to be a major player in bringing about these visits. They were with some of the people I love the most in my life.

Trust me when I tell you this was the first step in being prepared to receive the good news of the 'Forgiveness Letter' when I finally open it. You, being on the journey with me by reading my story has allowed you to see what that 'controlling and reordering the voice' led me to in my life. It will lead to the same place for you as you begin by embracing your newfound position in "The Rose" story.

I'm not a Doctor, Psychologist, Preacher, or Self-Help Guru. I'm not famous and I don't have a ton of New York Times Bestsellers. I am however a man who went searching and I discovered the path of life free of self-inflicted pain and suffering. Those things that combined with the voids and drugs to create 'My Perfect Storm of Addiction'. In writing this book I found an amazing tool to do just that. I found the Power of Forgiveness. In discovering this I also found self-worth. I no longer crave the vices I once did to fill the void of not loving myself and others, because I now love myself, as God loves me.

This may sound like a little kid's nursery rhyme yet; it is in reality a big kid's lifeline. My lifeline. Doubt and Fear can't hold a candle to the love that now exists within me. True love, not manufactured by the highs of drugs and alcohol. True love from the one who is Love. Despite the hate that can surround me at times, I hold true to His Power of Forgiveness put to work through me. Something I now catch myself activating on a daily basis. I have many opportunities within these prison walls, and you have many opportunities outside of them, right where you are. Remember this if you are to take away anything from coming on the journey of my life with me. There is nowhere on the planet that forgiveness can't be utilized. I'm unstoppable in its presence and so will you be.

My question to you my friend is the same one I hope I have prompted you to ask yourself. "What's stopping me from surrendering to The Power of Forgiveness?"

AFTERWORD

I, the 'Old Man', am now into the 20th year since the discovery of the Antidote for Addiction began its work in me. On that early September morning in a complete drunken stupor, I lay neatly tucked face up cocooned inside the twin bed my sister Lisa had spent most of her teenage years in. My widowed mother Ada slept, or maybe not, just on the other side of the wall in the same bedroom, she had spent 43 years in with my dad, Gerald. He had suffered for more years than that with the same thing I lay there suffering with that night, Addiction. Addiction to Alcohol.

He had not beaten it, tamed it, or been released from it, and neither had I. If countable we would have easily logged up collectively more than 10,000 failed attempts at it. Yet here I lay just awoken by something to find myself unable to move. I drank myself past the point of spinning hours before and lay there with almost no visible light staring at the ceiling when a question came to me, "How did I get tucked in so tight, with my arms completely inside the covers like this?" The tears began to flow immediately as the memory of being tucked in so tight as a child came back as if yesterday. Tucked in tight as a child in that very same bedroom that my brother and myself slept years before Lisa occupied it. Yet, I wasn't a child. I was the 45-year-old drunk man who had been tucked in tight by the same one who lovingly performed the task years before, Mom. I pulled my arms from the restraints of the blanket and put my hands over my face to block the sound of my cry, "What have I done? Oh, my God, no?" With that, the memory of what had transpired brought more horror than the revelation of the cocoon. I saw myself earlier being so drunk that I knew I couldn't walk up the stairs without tripping, falling, or making so much noise I would wake the only other occupant of the house, Mom. I had decided to crawl up them but made it only 10 steps when the door at the top opened and I saw her standing in shock at what she was staring back at. She reached down to help me. In total fear I knew full well that if I attempted to reach up for her, we would both be at the bottom in an instant, probably killing her. I then remember telling her to back up and let me be. As I crawled in front of her in the hallway, she closed the door and then reached down saying, "Let's get you off to bed?" The next recollection that came flooding back as I lay there was, is, and will remain the defining image that represents the changing point of my Alcohol Addiction. As she was bent over working to finish tucking me in, I had closed my eyes pretending I had passed out so as not to be confronted by her. As she had done so many nights, so many years ago when I was a little boy, when she finished at my shoulders, she kissed me on the forehead and whispered, "I love you." That memory crushed me beyond repair.

Crying and shaking I put my hands up in the air toward the ceiling and said "Dear God I cannot do this anymore. This is so much bigger than I am, or ever will be. Please, please, please take it from me. Forgive me for being such a fool. Please!?" I closed my eyes still crying and passed out.

A couple of hours later the sound of a coffee cup hitting a counter snapped me awake. It took me a good 20 seconds to recognize where I was, and when I did the memory of the whole night and early morning reflection, surrender, and plea came flooding back. The fact that I was not in the least hungover surprised me. What surprised me more was that I felt no condemnation for what I had done. Condemnation had always been the first thought that came along with my endless hangovers, yet it didn't exist this morning. Instead, it was as if the guilt of it were already in the past and there was a task that lay ahead for me. I rolled out on my knees reliving the prayer position I had been commanded to take on that same floor every waking morning so many years ago. I simply said, "Dear God, thank you for this day, I will follow your lead into whatever is ahead," and rolled back up, got dressed, made the bed, and headed out to see the one who had tucked me in.

With the clearest of heads of the soberest of men, I walked into the kitchen where she had a cup of coffee waiting for me directly across from where she set. I deduced a 'Motherly Chat' was about to take place. As if I had been called to do so I walked over to her side, bent forward kissed her on the top of her head, and said, "Mom, I love you and I promise you that what took place last night will never ever happen again!" Turning I took my seat and a sip of coffee. Not speaking she stared for a few seconds straight into my eyes that were holding back tears. Then she grabbed her coffee and stood up. As if repeating my previous move, she stepped to my side, bent forward kissed the top of my head, and said "That will be nice. I'll always love you," then surprisingly walked off into her living room. No further 'Chat' was to come.

One thing that she had said caused me to sit there for a minute and ponder its meaning. I took it as I believed it was meant to be delivered. As a confirmation that today really was the day that drinking would be behind me. She had said "That *will* be nice," not "That *would* be nice." 'Will', seemed so full of expectation as if assured. Whereas 'would', seemed so full of only the possibility of reality. I chose to rest on what I heard her say, stood up and moved on into the new day that lay ahead.

That was going on 20 years ago this year. To this day not only have I never had another drink, craved another drink, obsessed over another drink, I have not and do not call myself an alcoholic or a recovering alcoholic.

In the days to follow when the issue arose, which with so many drinking friends happened often, I let them know the same thing I let my mother know, "This will never happen again." Their disbelief was understood as they had heard similar words from me for years. They did not yet realize there was something different going on behind those words. Heck at the time I couldn't really describe it as I was still in a bit of amazement myself. Yet, over time I realized exactly what it was. And what it wasn't. It wasn't a mask, or a 'live with-it' training system, or a coping method or an accepting 'as is' method. It didn't have twelve steps, though it had a few. It wasn't a daily reminder of my past failings as if still lived.

What it was is a daily reminder of my deliverance from a past that did not have a place in my present. It was a daily growth in the renewal of my mind to the new place of truth. It was a daily reminder of my life in the present where alcohol wasn't 'necessary' therefore presented no allure or attraction. That was gone. Now, it can be gone for you too.

The keyword that I hope you see is 'deliverance'. This is what is to be expected from the antidote for addiction, deliverance. This is what I encouraged Cody to search for and discover. He fought me hard and had a few choice words for me when I refused to tell him what it was but encouraged him to keep digging. Keep searching. Keep looking. His story has hopefully taken you on the journey in discovering it with him, that you may now continue on the journey, your journey in discovering it in your story.

The antidote was injected into me that very morning that I lay freshly uncocooned in that bed. Its Power of deliverance came to me the moment that from my aching heart I said "Dear God I cannot do this anymore. This is so much bigger than I am, or ever will be. Please, please, please take it from me. Forgive me for being such a fool. Please!?" Remember, I didn't even realize what had taken place, yet it took place, nonetheless.

It was in that very moment that I was forgiven by the only One that could truly forgive me, once and for all, of the many transgressions my addiction had led me into over the previous 30 years. The debt I owed was too big for any living person or group to forgive. Yet, because He was the ultimate provider of forgiveness by offering us His Son, Jesus Christ to pay the debt for us, it came to pass for me.

With this position of deliverance and new internal spiritual forgiveness, I got a tugging to look into how and why I had fallen so deep into addiction.

I did a deep dive into my past to help solve a few things that puzzled me. I knew I had some things from my past and present that seemed to be kept at bay with my drinking. I felt compelled to see what the truth of them were and find a better path to resolve them, to find happiness and peace in my life. There were things that I felt I needed to prove were either true or false.

In the process, I was shocked to discover things that were but a figment of my imagination. Many were a mental creation for what I felt were made up for my own promotion or protection. Some things were simply just false, but I had accepted them as true for so long that they became as if really true. I made many bad decisions based on them. Then I found that there were things that were simply just true, but I had accepted them as false for so long that they had become as if really false. I made some bad decisions based on them also. Yet, most of all I found out that many people's roles in painful events surrounding those truths and falsehoods could not be changed. Those people whose actions had hurt me and my own actions that had hurt other people. It seemed the only resolve would be some sort of forgiveness because I couldn't change them and couldn't live with the pain from them. I began by recognizing my own forgiveness, then set out to model that. I believed I could not wait for people to change before I forgave them. The only way for it to be a permanent release was to give it over to the same One who took it from me, God. When I did it was instant and complete.

This was the point when I discovered the difference between what I call Intellectually Reasoned Forgiveness and Spiritually Graced Forgiveness. The first is the one that everyone says we need to do. Forgive because it is harmful to hold on. Harmful for you to continue to harbor the belief that someone owes you a debt for the transgressions they brought upon you. Knowing full well they have no intention of paying it. So, you decide to use your willpower to overcome it and say, "Screw it, I'm letting it go!" Or so you think you are. You make a mental list and put the list of debts from the infractions in your back pocket, out of sight, out of mind. All goes along just fine, and the relationship is now tolerable, manageable, and in some cases growing. And then all of a sudden, a little infraction happens. Instantly instead of seeing and reacting as if it is a brand new, never happened before infraction, you reach into your back pocket and pull out the old ones. This little infraction is now huge because it gets tacked on in your mind as infraction #21! You find yourself in worse shape than when you first forgave and the need for debt repayment comes back now full-on into your psyche. You live with it until you can tolerate it no more and once again say "Screw it, I'm letting it go, again!" This type of forgiveness when used and free of new infractions is wonderful. But, as anyone who has lived a life cycle of these will tell you they are troublesome at best, and destructive at worse because they rely on the good behavior of others. And those others, like ourselves, struggle to always be on their best behavior. That is Intellectually Reasoned Forgiveness. I used this type until it was revealed to me that there was another, permanent type available.

Spiritually Graced Forgiveness is the type that God used on me. I knew full well I owed a debt for all I had done. A really big debt. I knew I was struggling to find better behaviors that wouldn't continue to add to the debt I owed. Yet, right in the middle of all that, someone was willing to forgive me without me paying the debt, by allowing someone else to pay it for me. I wasn't deserving of it, but someone did it anyway. When someone does that physically, mentally, or spiritually it is called grace. Grace being "unmerited favor given". It is one of the rarest types of forgiveness on earth, but it is the only type that comes from God. Jesus Christ is that very Grace. That is the One type of forgiveness I was introduced to from my drunken stupor in that bed all those years ago. I did not deserve it, but it came nonetheless because I called out to God for it.

It took me quite some time to discover that the same permanent Spiritually Graced Forgiveness was available to be used by me with others in my life. Years to make the transition from one to the other. But when I did the full power of that Antidote for Addiction began to play out in every area of my life. God had allowed the debt of my infractions to go to Christ and be no more. I had finally realized He also allowed me to take the debt of infractions against me by others to Christ and be no more as well. When that happened the pain of the debt disappeared. This is Spiritually Grace Forgiveness. It is available to you and for you.

A few years after that first Antidote morning I found a book called "The Alcohol and Addiction Cure" by Prentis. Knowing I had been cured and how I had gone about it, I was curious to see how they would teach me how to achieve it. When I arrived at Chapter 5, page 145 I was amazed to find that I had indeed years earlier addressed many of the same underlying true/false reasonings for my addiction. They had come to me without previously reading of them, yet here they were now in print in front of me as I read. Wow!

I had been on a journey of discovery that modeled what Prentis had journeyed and discovered, with but one difference. I had used Spiritually Graced Forgiveness and not just Intellectually Reasoned Forgiveness.

You have now joined Cody on his journey of the same discovery. You have felt his pain and had pain of your own arise as you have traveled. You have been able to witness how he has navigated the things that popped up along the way of which some were even of his own making. You have seen how he once resisted and hesitated to even look at it, then go on to face it, encounter it, embrace it, and receive it, the Antidote for Addiction, forgiveness.

He has laid this all before you in the snapshot of the story of his life. You recognize that he is still on the journey as I was after my own discovery. This is a wonderful thing. This is the way it is supposed to be.

My hope for you is that in all that you have read you recognize the most important thing of all, you, and your relationship with God! That you recognize as you reach the end of this book you are in actuality reaching the end of the new 'Chapter #1' of your own story. The story of what has happened to you physically, emotionally, and spiritually while on this journey is your 'Chapter # 2' or return to life as you knew it prior to picking up this book. One thing is for sure, no matter which direction you go, you are not the same as before. You have been pricked in your spirit whether you believe it or not, by the very One that caused you to pick up the book in the first place, God. He will guide you as to your next step as you seek the Antidote for yourself. When the decision is made, and you cry out like I did that early morning twenty years ago there will be nothing that will get in your way that is insurmountable. Nothing!

The 'Old Man' that challenged Cody to enter and stay the course is now challenging you to the same. I challenge you to not turn back. Let this be your time. Do not let that voice of negativity that drove Cody down the darker path have a place in your thoughts. Cast that un-holy, un-healthy spirit aside and free up room for the Holy, Healthy Spirit voice of God to be heard. Reach up, and reach out, there is a myriad of doors waiting to be opened just for you. It all begins right now with your belief in God's belief in you. There is nothing Greater. You are, always were, and remain 'The Rose'! Stand in that truth and take the next steps Cody has put before you. Soon you will grow into that belief in yourself and continue to live in and take actions for the abundant peace of life you seek. Forgiven and freed of addiction by the True Antidote, Spiritually Graced Forgiveness.

God's Peace on your way.

Gary Martel, the 'Old Man'

CONGRATULATIONS!

Way to go!

You made it on the journey with Cody through
Surviving The Perfect Storm of Addiction.

Don't Stop Now!
Don't Turn Back!

We encourage you to continue on Your Personal Journey
from your arrival right here, right now.

Continue to live out this New Direction for you, your life, and or
the life of the 'loved one' who has been on your mind throughout.

Turn the page and discover how it is possible for you to
Survive That Perfect Storm of Addiction.

Your life will never, can never, be the same.

WHAT NEXT?

THE TRANSITION FROM CODY'S STORY TO YOURS!

Let Your Chapter #2 begin right here, right now. Whether you are one who is, like Cody & Gary once were, personally caught up in the throes of Addiction or if you are one that has taken this journey in order to better understand the face of addiction and help a loved one, we encourage you to take the next step…Pray…

"Dear God, Thank You for having me read and witness Your Spiritually Graced Forgiveness, completing the first Chapter of my own journey to deliverance and freedom. I am asking You, right here right now for this very forgiveness over me (over the life of my loved one) who suffers from the un-holy, un-healthy voice of addiction. May you reveal to me the Grace from which this comes. May you open my heart to hear Your Voice that I may Trust in You to be positioned In You to receive Your deliverance. I am ready. In Jesus Name, Amen."

If you *'did'* pray that prayer, then go to www.antidoteforaddiction.com and click on *My Chapter #2.* You will find the Support, Direction, Instruction, and Guidance for 'living delivered' from that which once bound you. Remember this; You are not alone, God's got you. God Believes in you. We believe in you.

If you *'did not'* pray that prayer, for whatever reason, fear not, the unholy, unhealthy spirit will not prevail as you go to www.antidoteforaddiction.com and click on *Completing My Chapter #1*. You will find the Support, Direction, Instruction, and Guidance on how to defeat that which is attempting to keep you bound. Remember this; You are not alone, God's got you. God Believes in you. We believe in you.

If you '*feel paralyzed*' to do either and still have questions in any area of your addiction and its stronghold on your life, go to www.antidoteforaddition.com and click on *FAQs* (frequently asked questions). You will even find a place to 'type in' any unasked question that you don't find. Remember this; You are not alone, God's got you. God Believes in you. We believe in you.

May God's Peace be with you on Your Journey.

We look forward to seeing, hearing, and experiencing the Journey Of Your Blessed Life.

ABOUT THE AUTHOR

Cody Lanus is an Iowa native, raised in Omaha Nebraska, and moved on to attend High School and College in the Kansas City, Missouri area. He worked hard mentally and physically, ascending to become a Star Athlete in multiple sports with his Highest Achievements in High School and College Football. Many who were in the stands will still remember his name today. His powerful, compelling, moving story of his descent from that high position into a world of drugs, and how he 'Survived the Perfect Storm of Addiction' is written within these pages. His hope and prayer are that telling his story may help you or a loved one do just the same. Cody is currently serving out a 12-year prison sentence where he found himself while riding in the middle of that 'Perfect Storm.'

ABOUT THE 'OLD MAN'

Gary Martel was 'called' to turn his six-year experience as a 'white-collar' prisoner, and the revelations of the deep study into the core forces within himself that led him there, into the *PriscillAquila Enterprise*.

This is where he met Cody Lanus.

He is now the founder, grantor, and facilitator of this ***Christian 'Business Missions' Development Company***. He is the Host of Seminars, Webinars, Workshops, and Mastermind Groups made available through the *PriscillAquila Institute* and He hosts the weekly *PriscillAquila Power Podcast* covering an array of topics that impact Christian 'Business Missions' Entrepreneurs, Employees, and Ministries. Their mission is in 'Bringing 1st Century Christian Principles Alive in Business Today' via the *PriscillAquila Ministry*. It feeds one of the greatest under-served Christian Missionary fields today, the field of Business.

Gary is also the author of two creative non-fiction manuscripts, 'Thirty Years in the Wilderness' and 'Fifty Years A Thief' which are currently in the pre-publication phase with the *PriscillAquila Press* the publisher of the new release of ***"TATTOOS"***.

BIBLIOGRAPHY

Greg Bishop, *The Logan Effect*, Sports Illustrated March 11,2019, Page 66.

Tupac Shakur, *Hail Mary*, Universal Music Corporation, February 11, 1997.

Brandon Boyd, Incubus, *Wish You Were Here*, Epic, August 14,2001.

Chris Prentis, *The Alcohol and Addiction Cure*, Power Press, 2007, Page 145

The Holy Bible, *King James Version*, Thomas Nelson Inc. 1982

CPSIA information can be obtained
at www.ICGtesting.com
Printed in the USA
LVHW011655270821
696219LV00007B/112